Digital
Copyright Protection

Digital
Copyright Protection

Peter Wayner

AP PROFESSIONAL

AP PROFESSIONAL is a division of Academic Press

Boston   San Diego   New York
London   Sydney   Tokyo   Toronto

This book is printed on acid-free paper. ∞
Copyright © 1997 by Academic Press

AP PROFESSIONAL
1300 Boylston St, Chestnut Hill, MA 02167
http://www.apnet.com/approfessional

An Imprint of ACADEMIC PRESS
A division of HARCOURT BRACE & COMPANY

United Kingdom Edition published by
ACADEMIC PRESS LIMITED
24-28 Oval Road, London NW1 7DX, UK
http://www.hbuk.co.uk/ao/

Library of Congress Cataloging-in-Publication Data

Wayner, Peter,
    Digital copyright protection / Peter Wayner.
        p.   cm.
    Includes bibliographical references and index.
    ISBN 0-12-788771-7 (alk. paper)
    1. Computer security. 2. Data protection. 3. Copyright and electronic
data processing. 4. Copyright infringement. I. Title.
QA76.9.A25W39   1997
005.8—dc21   97-14004
                                                                  CIP

Printed in the United States of America
98 99 00 01 02 CP 9 8 7 6 5 4 3 2

Contents

Preface

Much of the information in this book was built upon my knowledge of how to hide information in plain sight. My greatest source of information comes from the various contributors to the Cypherpunks mailing list who manage to inject some quality information into a turbulent, boiling stream of debate. I would like to thank everyone who's managed to contribute to this list and the newsgroup `sci.crypt` over the years.

Bruce Schneier was kind enough to give me an electronic version of the bibliography from his first book. [Sch94] I converted it into Bibtex format and used it for some of the references here. Ross Anderson's annotated bibliography on Information Hiding was also a great help.

The team of people at AP Professional were incredibly gracious with their time and encouragement. I'm glad for all of their support through this manuscript. They are: Jeff Pepper, Mike Williams, Julie Champagne, Barbara Northcott, and Tom Ryan.

There were others who helped in the world beyond the text. The staff at Tax Analysts was kind enough to coordinate my consulting schedule with the demands of putting out a book. Anyone would be lucky to work for a company that was so understanding. My editors at *BYTE* and the *New York Times* have been very willing to bend their schedules around the needs of producing this book.

Finally, I want to thank everyone in my family for everything they've given through all of my life.

Peter Wayner, Baltimore, MD, April 1997
`pcw@access.digex.com`
`http://access.digex.net:/~pcw/pcwpage.html`

Book Notes

The copy for this book was typeset using the LaTeX typesetting software. Several important breaks were made with standard conventions in order to remove some ambiguities. The period mark is normally included inside the quotation marks like this: "That's my answer. No. Period." This can cause ambiguities when computer terms are included in quotation marks because computers often use periods to convey some meaning. For this reason, my electronic mail address is "pcw@access.digex.com". Almost all periods are left outside of the quotation marks to prevent confusion.

Chapter 1

Copyright Battles

This chapter introduces the notion of defending copyright in an era of easy reproduction. It outlines the two major solutions (encryption and watermarking) and maps out the advantages and disadvantages of using them.

The best place to begin in this book is with the bad news: there is no absolute way to prevent people from copying the digital versions of your text, your music, your movie, or your data. If a computer will interpret the data and let someone use it, then that same computer can be programmed to grab the data and make a copy of it. The flexibility and programmability of these machines are a double-edged sword. Creating new works is substantially easier with word processors, sound editors, and other multimedia tools, but the cost is living in a world where the copyright infringers have the same advantages.

Despite this fundamental truth, there are some techniques that can make life more complicated for copyright infringers. The approaches can still be circumvented by the smartest programmers and users, but this task can be onerous enough to make it easier for someone to simply buy another copy instead of trying to steal it. The technology may not be strong enough on its own, but it can join with the forces of economics to stop most attacks.

This book describes a number of different techniques for making life difficult for the would-be infringers. At the simplest level, they can be divided into two parts. The first is to require special software for displaying the information upon the screen. This software, of course, comes with no save feature that would make a copy. These systems are often not strong enough on their own and they must be combined with access to a trusted oracle that dispenses the secret key for unlocking the data.

There are three types of oracles: local ones built into tamperproof hardware, distant ones accessed through toll-free numbers, and networked ones reached through the Internet. Each one has its own set of advantages and can be a reasonable part of controlling the flow of information.

The second major technique is to make each copy of a document unique by embedding some personalization tag. If an illicit copy is found, perhaps for sale in Hong Kong, the tag can be recovered and the original owner identified. These tags can be embedded in a subtle fashion where it may be impossible to detect them.

The game is largely a job of hide and seek. If the tags are spotted, then the infringer may try to remove them. Each algorithm has its specific weaknesses. Some are easier to detect and others are easier to remove. No algorithm is perfect, especially if the infringer is willing to tolerate some significant change in the data in order to ensure that all of the tags are removed.

Locked Boxes

The process of shipping data in a digital version of the locked box created with encryption algorithms is one solution to copy proliferation. The data can travel through any cheap channel and then the user can pay for the key to unlock it. Pirates may be able to grab a copy made through the cheap channel, but they won't be able to use it because they don't have the key. Here are some of the different types of locking used:

CD-ROMs These disks are very cheap to make in quantity and hold a relatively large amount of information. It is easy to deliver a lot of data to people, but it is expensive to customize that data. One solution is to produce a CD-ROM containing copies of all the data, but encrypt each piece of data with an individual key. An individual can get a customized set by just getting the right keys.

This solution may be best used in the graphics arts business, where Adobe sells a disk with a huge selection of fonts for a relatively low price. Each font is encrypted individually and artists must buy the key to each font if they want to use them.

Text Boxes Several companies (IBM and InterTrust) are building systems to lock up documents in encrypted files. A separate application will display the information after communicating with some central server that dispenses the keys. These keys must be available anytime someone may want to read an article.

This scheme also offers the possibility for sophisticated royalty payment because the copyright holder would, for the first time, have access to when someone reads information. Some user may, for instance, get a kickback for recommending a particular article to a friend. When the friend reads the piece, the central office notes this and passes a share back. The number of schemes is limited only by the creativity of the marketing staff.

Special Tape Decks The movie and music businesses are both embracing copy protection schemes that may have a limited ability to stop casual copying among consumers. These decks watch for a special signal that says, "Do not copy" and then obey it.

Satellite Television The satellite television systems encrypt their signals. Users must have special smart cards containing the decoding keys. These systems also offer sophisticated pay-per-view options that permit them to turn on individual boxes after the user has paid for a particular event.

Cable Television Pay-per-view systems on conventional U.S. cable systems will scramble the signal. If a customer purchases the show, then the cable company sends an unlocking signal to the person's box, which then descrambles the channel.

The main advantage of locking systems is that they allow most of the data to be distributed through a slow, cheap medium. The unlocking key is the only part that needs to be delivered when someone has the need for the data.

Tagging Data

Many of the algorithms in this book are devoted to inserting some form of tagging data into an image or a sound file. This tagging data can be used to either identify the true copyright holder or even identify the rightful owner of a particular copy of the data. Tagging each copy of a document may seem radical in the era of the fixed plate printing press, but it is becoming increasingly easy to do as computers become stronger and stronger.

The tagging data can also be used for other ancillary purposes beyond copy protection. Some users are tagging parts of images to identify their contents. Green grass gets a tag "grass" to help photo researchers catalog the images and locate images with particular contents. This idea is in its infancy, but it could also have applications in helping the blind "see" an image or helping people learn a new language.

Another possible use of the tagging data is preventing modification. The tagging data could be arranged in such a way that any change or alteration of the data would reveal a change in the tagging data and thus a change in the document.

None of the tagging schemes are perfect, but they can offer a good amount of security against the unaware. Here are some of the major solutions:

Changing the Noise There are many ways to add small changes to a document in such a way that it won't be easily detected by the naked eye or ear. These small changes can carry information that only a computer would notice. The user would not be able to tell the difference between the usual noise and hiss that may be present and a special tag carrying unique information. One of the simplest solutions is flipping the least significant bits in an image or an audio file.

In an ordinary decimal number like 1234, the least significant digit is the last one, "4". The same concept holds when the number is stored in binary.

This approach can be limited by the effects of some compression algorithms that produce good compression by cutting corners. These are called "lossy" because they do not reproduce the data exactly, but they come close. Coming close is not good enough when the noise contains important copyright information. This process can be mitigated by error-correcting codes, but it can't be avoided.

Changing Words Many words have synonyms and many phrases can be restated in a slightly different form. Information can be hidden by making these changes. Of course, this approach is limited by the structure of language. Mark Twain said that the difference between the right word and the word that is almost right is the same as the difference between lightning and a lightning bug.

Adding Waves Many image processing and audio processing techniques involve viewing the data as a set of superimposed waves. Changing the amplitude of the waves can add a nice amount of tagging information without distorting the appearance of the data. These techniques are similar to the amplitude and frequency modulation used in AM or FM radios.

Many lossy compression algorithms use wave-based techniques that use waves to model the data. Using similar wave-based techniques to inject tagging information will often survive the compression losses because the waves used to model the data for compression will also pick up the wave-based tagging information.

Necessary Features

There are a number of desirable features for tagging data:

Unobtrusiveness The tagging data should be undetectable by the casual viewer. No one should be able to notice any degradation in the quality of the signal because of the tagging. Consumers often justify "removing" the copy protection signal from VCR tapes because it hurts the quality. An imperceptible system does not provide this excuse.

Tamper Resistance There should be no easy way for a hacker to remove the tagging data. This resistance can take several forms:

Unlocatable The tagging information may be simple, but it may be randomly distributed among the data. There is no easy way to identify which pixels or parts of the data contribute to the tag so there is no simple way to remove the tag.

Inseparable The tagging information may not be removed without degrading the quality of the image by a significant amount. Many of the spread-spectrum wave techniques embed the information in a large fraction of the data. Destroying the tagging information means changing this large fraction, which can significantly degrade the image.

Unblendable One simple attack can be mounted if more than one copy of the data is available. If there are two copies with different tags, then it may be possible to either average the two or interleave the two in such a way that the tagging bits from both copies are destroyed. Many of the spread-spectrum techniques can avoid this approach and they often reveal the tagging elements of both copies. This allows both sources to be identified.

Resistant to Errors Many signals may be changed slightly by transmission and many more are changed by lossy compression systems like JPEG or MPEG. A good tagging scheme will still display the data even after the image has been compressed and reconstituted.

Segmentable Both audio and visual signals may be cut or cropped. A good tagging scheme will still produce the data from fragments. This requires that the information be repeated throughout the sample and the coding scheme must be able to recover from a cropped image.

Distortion Resistant Both audio and visual signals may be purposely distorted for artistic effects. Sound engineers may add qualities like reverb. Visual images may be distorted by some affine transformation in the process. Also many techniques used for blending and color correction may change the data in the image. A great tagging scheme can resist these effects.

None of the tagging schemes described in this book can satisfy all of these requirements, but there are some that can satisfy each of them. To a large extent, there are a number of tradeoffs between the different requirements. Some of the schemes become more tamper-resistant if a stronger setting is used, but this stronger setting also makes greater changes in the images and makes the existence of the tagging data more self-evident. Often, more resistance means more distortion.

Copyright Infrastructure

The focus of this book is largely on technical solutions to restrict copyright infringers. Each solution, however, brings with it some cost. The tradeoff between cost and protection takes many forms:

Ownership Registries If the copyrighted data is tagged with the identity of the rightful owner, then the copyright holder must keep some record of the sale and the contract between the owner and the copyright holder. This database will allow them to track down the person if an extra copy is found to have been created illegally.

Privacy Any large record of who reads what, who listens to what or who watches which movie is bound to send shivers up the spines of anyone who cares about their privacy. The downside of tagging data with the rightful owner is that the owner is forced to acknowledge reading that information. The full effects of such a widespread system for monitoring artistic consumption are not known, but it is hard to imagine any good results.

Real-time Infrastructure Some systems require the user's computer to acquire a key to decode the data before displaying it on the screen. The payment is made at this time. Any company that wants to offer this service must be prepared to keep a computer attached to the Internet with the ability to dispense these keys. Ideally, accessing information through these encrypted packages should be just as easy as picking up a document. This can happen only if the infrastructure is put in place.

Electronic Payment Mechanisms At the time of this writing, the credit card industry is the only one offering any simple mechanism for transferring money over the Internet. Several companies, however, are actively exploring payment mechanisms that have significantly lower transaction costs. This book does not focus on these digital cash systems (see my other book, *Digital Cash*, also published by AP Professional), but any company that wants to sell information over the Internet should actively explore them. Dispensing the information quickly requires getting payment quickly.

Real-time Tagging If the data is going to be tagged with personalized information about the owner, then this job will need to be done quickly. Most of the algorithms described in the book can be executed by an average computer in a short amount of time. More sophisticated algorithms, however, may need a larger infrastructure.

The tagging process also places some limitations on reselling. Many data owners may sell copies of their data through multiple venues. Any real-time tagging system may be difficult to administer in these situations, especially if the data is being resold under another brand name.

Legal Difficulties The process of litigating copyright infringement is complicated because there are lawyers involved. The law in the United States makes a big practical distinction between copying something for commercial gain and merely copying it for personal use. The definition of fair use is also filled with many ambiguous areas. It is not clear, for instance, how much text is permissible to quote.

Tagged data offers the ability to trace a copy back to the person who bought a copy of the information. This may or may not produce enough practical evidence to prosecute the person. The copy may have been stolen before the copy was made, for instance. The tags, however, are enough to offer a serious impediment to any large-scale copyright infringement process. If a copyright holder discovered that one person has repeatedly "lost" copies, then it would provide a much stronger case. This would force any copyright infringer to use different channels.

Copyright Enforcement If tagged data is available on the network, then it may be possible to use network scanning tools like web-crawlers to look for copyright infringement. A popular web-crawling site like Alta Vista (`www.altavista.digital.com`) or Infoseek (`www.infoseek.com`) may choose to also scan for tags in images, movies, or audio data while it is building its index. They could download each image and record its rightful owner. Any copyright holder could use this database to track infringers. Such a service would probably charge copyright holders separately because it would involve a significant new investment. The current machines do not search images and this saves them time. Images are often much larger than the accompanying text.

Text, on the other hand, may be tracked with conventional web-crawling index builders. Some chapters in this book describe how to change the words and phrases embedded in each version of the text. The current scanners can all watch for particular phrases and if the phrases are rare enough, they can be used to narrow the search to a manageable level.

Each of these details is a significant part of the equation that copyright holders must use to determine how to protect their work. Choosing to enforce a digital copyright has significant costs that must be balanced against the increased revenues. Many of the techniques in this book may be economically infeasible for small producers who don't generate much revenues. But they could be very important for any company with a product that can generate enough revenues to pay for the cost.

The techniques in this book are too new to offer any solid guidance or revenue models. Much of the success will depend on the cost of maintaining a presence on the Internet. The cost of this is declining rapidly as the tools for custom programming become better developed. It is relatively easy now to receive requests, query a database, and return an answer in a short amount of time. The big question is whether keeping the publisher in the loop is worth the extra revenues.

Terms in the Book

This book tries to use terms in a consistent manner. The word *data*, when it is unmodified by an adjective, usually refers to the copyrighted work that the owner is trying to protect. It may be audio, visual, textual or some combination of all three. A *tag* is a block of information or data that is placed in the copyrighted material, often in an imperceptible manner. It may include information about the copyright holder, the terms of use, or unique information about the rightful license holder for a particular copy. It may also be called the *tagging information*.

The word *encryption* applies to all attempts to make data inscrutable to anyone who doesn't have the proper *key*, which in the digital domain is just another collection of bits. Some algorithms have one key, known as the *secret key*, and these are often referred to as *symmetric key* encryption or even plain *encryption*. Others have two keys known as the *public key* and the *private key* and they are often referred to as *asymmetric encryption* or *public key encryption*.

The *public key encryption* algorithms can also be used to create *digital signatures*. These are popular options that can be used by someone to verify the authenticity of a block of data.

The process of hiding information where it may not be visible is often called *steganography*. The 1996 Conference on Information Hiding produced a set of agreed upon terms to clarify the domain [Pfi96]. In this document, *embedded data* or *embedded message* refers to the data hidden inside the *cover text*, *cover image*, or *cover sound file*. The result is often called the *stegotext* or *stegoimage*. This is meant to act as a counterpart to the popular terms, *plaintext* and *cryptext*, which refer to a message before and after it was encrypted.

Someone trying to defeat a copyright protection scheme may be called an *attacker*. If the scheme uses encryption to lock away data, then that person may be called a *cryptanalyst* practicing *cryptanalysis*. If the scheme hides tagging information from sight, then that person may be called a *steganalyst* practicing *steganalysis*.

In this book, the concept of a *tag* is generally meant to refer to the information embedded in data. The cover text is generally the copyrighted work.

Structure of the Book

There are three different types of chapters in this book. The chapters at the beginning of the book build a foundation of general techniques that can help many different algorithms. Cryptography and coding theory are some of the more important tools. These topics are offered only as an introduction and more complete information can be found in books devoted to the topics.

The second class of chapters deals with specific approaches for copyright protection. These include encrypting the data and adding tags. There are different chapters for adding tags to images, text, and sound files. Some of these chapters offer more specific approaches for adding tagging data to all three. These chapters are aimed at people who want a thorough understanding of the different algorithms and may be willing to undertake the development of their own software.

The third class of chapters describes some of the commercial products on the market. These commercial products often provide the best solution for basic users because the companies are concentrating on providing turnkey solutions. The world of copyright protection is fairly new right now and many companies are just beginning to bring products to market. For these reasons, the fast changes in the marketplace may mean that not all products are covered.

Many chapters begin with an allegorical, potentially humorous, exploration of the topic at hand. These are intended to provide another, slightly skewed, approach to the topic in the hope of better explaining and illustrating the topic. The rest of the chapter is devoted to providing a more technical explanation.

How to Use This Book

Many people may find a need to explore the field of copyright defense. Some might be publishing executives who want to get a high-level view of some solutions. Others may be programmers or technical staff with the job of implementing the solutions. This book can help both the readers with a casual need and those who want details. Here's a list of solutions:

Publishing Executive Read this introductory chapter. Read the introductory sections of the basic chapters to get a good understanding of the buzzwords. Skim the allegorical sections of the technical chapters to get a high-level feeling for what is going on. Peruse the chapters devoted to products you're interested in using.

Programmer Read every part in depth.

Cryptographer Many of the techniques described for hiding tagging data can also be used to send surreptitious messages. The technology for tagging each copy of a document can also be used to hide information and communication from prying eyes.

Chapter 2

Cryptography

Cryptography is a major tool for locking up information or enforcing authenticity. This chapter provides a high-level introduction to the topic as background and suggests how the various tools can be used effectively.

The science of cryptography is one of the most powerful tools for protecting copyright. It gives anyone the ability to lock up digital data so it can't be read without a key. It also provides a solid method for establishing the identity of a person and proving the authenticity of a request. Both of these solutions can be mixed and matched to develop different schemes for copyright protection.

This book is not a book about cryptography, per se. Some of the best books are fat enough. It would not be possible to cover cryptography in enough depth to compete against them. This chapter only summarizes some of the major algorithms and describes how they can be used to defend a copyright. If you want more detail, some of the best books include *Applied Cryptography* by Bruce Schneier [Sch94] and *Contemporary Cryptography* by Gus Simmons [ed.92].

The technology is one of the most important parts of the foundation of the Net and a solid infrastructure is developing around it. Many system developers can license libraries that do most of the work for you. This is often a good idea. The subject is vast and the mathematics is complicated. If you intend to experiment with encryption, it helps to study it in depth. I think that it, more than any other subject

I know, epitomizes Alexander Pope's dictum that "a little knowledge is a dangerous thing." Many system designers who have used cryptographic algorithms have left behind holes because they didn't fully understand the field.

Of course, government regulations are another major problem for people using cryptography. The U.S. government in particular feels that it must stop the export of any sufficiently powerful encryption software because it might be used by terrorists or enemies of the United States. This restriction should prove to be particularly onerous and unexpected to publishers and other copyright holders who are not used to thinking of themselves as international arms dealers. But such is the law. Publishing on paper is considered protected speech covered by the First Amendment to the U.S. Constitution. Publishing electronically and encrypting the data to control dissemination is legally indistinguishable from terrorism.

At this writing, the U.S. government is pushing some attempts at a "compromise." Companies will be able to export useful encryption algorithms if they equipped them with some "backdoor" that the government can use to examine the contents. Some people feel that this backdoor is an ideal way to allow the law enforcement officials to conduct surveillance and catch lawbreakers. Others view it as a real weakness that will eventually be exploited by an adversary.

The arguments over the export of cryptography continue to rage in the United States. There are many different proposals and counterproposals that frequently change, but the current limitations have remained pretty much the same. If you intend to use cryptographic protection on your copyrighted works and you intend to export this data, then you should maintain a close watch on changing regulation. Although not much has changed in any practical sense, there is so much discussion that something may happen.

Introduction to Cryptography

There is a wide range of cryptographic algorithms that are available. Some lock up data in a mathematical vault. Others produce signatures that guarantee a document's authenticity. Still others can be used to check for changes.

Many of them use a *key* to protect data. This key is just a long number. The encryption algorithms won't function unless you produce the right key. Anything else produces gibberish. It is a good idea to think of a key as a lever for the memory. Just as a mechanical lever allows you to move a heavy object with a smaller force, encryption with a key allows you to protect a large volume of data by remembering a small amount, the key.

This key must still be protected if you want to protect the data. Encryption is a relatively easy subject. The algorithms are well understood and relatively easy to implement. Key distribution, on the other hand, is complicated. Keys are still often distributed in advance through trusted couriers. They are later used to recover data.

The length of a key is often taken as a measure of its strength. Longer keys have more potential values and that means that someone must expend more time trying all possible keys looking for the right one. This is known as a "brute force" attack and it is the least sophisticated attack possible. It is not a good idea to rely on this as the ultimate judge of an algorithm's strength. A algorithm may have a long key but still be easy to break. The newspaper Cryptoquip puzzles that scramble the letters of a quotation might be said to have a key of 150 bits (6×25), but they're easy to break. DES has a key of 56 bits and it is much harder to break, although it is clear that its useful life is ending.

Here's a list of the some of the most important types of encryption and a description of how they can be used to protect copyrighted material:

Private Key Encryption This is the classic form of encryption. There is one key and both sides must possess a copy of it to access the data. Some of the most common private key algorithms are DES (Data Encryption Standard)[4677, 46-88], IDEA [Mei94], Blowfish [Sch94], RC-4, and Khufu [Mer91]. Each of these takes a key and locks up private data.

The major advantage of private key algorithms is that they're generally fast. Each of these has been optimized to provide the maximum amount of scrambling in a small number of calculations. Some of the algorithms, like DES, were optimized for electronic circuits. Others, like Blowfish, were optimized for general CPUs.

These algorithms are best used to lock up copyrighted data with a key. This key can be distributed later to allow someone to access the data. For instance, a CD-ROM can be pressed containing more than 600 megabytes of data. The copyright holder can, at a later date, reveal the keys to certain blocks of the data.

Public Key Encryption These algorithms use two keys. One is used for encrypting in the information and the other is used for decrypting it. The big difference is that the one used for encryption is useless for decrypting. This asymmetry allows two clever solutions. The first is to eliminate many of the key distribution hassles. A person can create a *public key pair* and publish one of the keys in an electronic phone book. If someone wants to send that person a message, then they can look up the public key and use it to encrypt the message. Now, only the secret key can be used to decrypt the message. If the person did a good job of keeping it secret, then no one can read the data coming to him.

The other neat result of the asymmetry is the *digital signature*. In some public key systems, the person can use the secret key to encrypt a message. Anyone who knows the matching public key can decrypt it, but only the person who knows the secret key could have generated that encrypted packet of data. Digital signature algorithms give each person a pair of keys and keep their secret half hidden on their hard disk. As long as the secret half remains secret, then no one can forge the signature.

The most popular public key algorithm is RSA [RSA78, RSA79] named after the three MIT scientists who developed it: Ron Rivest, Adi Shamir, and Len Adleman. The software is patented, but the main patent runs out soon [RSA83]. The patents are held by Public Key Partners, but a sister company, RSA Data Security, has put a substantial amount of time and effort into commercializing the algorithm. This is one reason why it is one of the most popular solutions around. There are many other public key algorithms around, but they're beyond the scope of this book.

Public key algorithms are quite useful in copyright protection. Forgeries and modified documents can be a problem in many situations and digital signatures can prevent this from happening. If a valid digital signature is attached to a document, then the reader can be certain that it is the same document produced by the person. This guarantee is much stronger than a personal signature made by a hand and a pen. It is easy to unbind a document, change a page, and insert it in the paper. A digital signature covers the entire document.

Public key encryption can also be used just like private key encryption to lock up data. The main advantage is that there can be some public directory of keys available to encrypt the data. The copyright holder may generate a private document by encrypting it so that it can be read only by the person holding the secret half of a key.

Hash Functions Hash functions take a big file and produce a small number that can be used as a surrogate for the file. Cryptographically secure hash functions do this in a way that can't be guessed. That is, it is practically impossible to find a file that generates a particular number.

Hash functions are often considered "poor man's" digital signatures. Many people who distribute material over the Internet publish the hash value of the data files in some public location. If you're worried about the authenticity, you can compute the hash function yourself and compare the values. If they're the same, then the file hasn't been modified. If they're different, then something has gone wrong. The "cryptographically secure" feature means that it would not be practical for someone to modify a file in a way that won't change the final hash value.

Some of the most important hash functions are MD-5 and a cousin, SHA (Secure Hash Algorithm). Both are used in many applications. The second, the SHA, is part of a U.S. government standard.

Copyright holders may want to use cryptographically secure hash functions to guard against changes in a document. They are much faster to compute than a public key signature and they are probably just as secure.

Subliminal Channels Many digital signature algorithms possess a *subliminal channel* that can be used to hide some additional information. These channels can be quite useful for copyright protection because they allow a copyright holder to personalize copies with the person's name. These tags cannot be practically altered because only the person who has the secret keys used to generate the signature can generate a new one. Chapter 3 describes these solutions in detail.

Time Stamping Hash functions and digital signatures can be mixed together to produce digital time stamps. One company, Surety Inc. (`www.surety.com`), offers a service and others could duplicate it.

This technique can be quite useful for copyright holders who want to produce some record of when a document exists. If there is a dispute between people over the copyright of a document, then one person could win the dispute by demonstrating that the person registered the document first. The time stamping algorithms are quite robust and powerful.

Bit Commitment One of the pleasures in life is being able to say, "I told you so." Unfortunately, in many cases this requires telling someone the details in advance and this may be practically impossible. For instance, stockbrokers may want to say, "I know a great stock that's guaranteed to go up." In order to prove themselves to a potential client, they would normally have to reveal the stock. No one would believe them if they revealed it afterward.

A bit commitment algorithm extends regular encryption. You can send the person an encrypted version of the document when you're making your bold prediction and then reveal the key later.

The rest of this chapter will provide specific examples of the different algorithms. It can't go into great detail without overwhelming the book. If you want more information, turn to either *Applied Cryptography* or *Contemporary Cryptography* for answers.

Private Key Encryption

The most important private key encryption algorithm of the last twenty years is the Data Encryption Standard. It was developed by IBM with some assistance by the National Security Agency. IBM published the algorithm and submitted it to the National Bureau of Standards (now National Institute of Standards and Technology), which validated it to keep unclassified data secure.

The algorithm was also one of the most influential and many people who designed algorithms after it imitated it in many ways. Algorithms like Khufu and Blowfish borrow major elements of its design. This is surprising, in some respects, because DES was initially greeted with some cynicism. Some of IBM's design criteria were classified and many suggested that the NSA may have worked to include a secret trapdoor. Later work by Eli Biham and Adi Shamir [BS91a, BS91b] showed that DES was actually stronger than its imitators and IBM later confirmed that this was one type of attack that was part of the classified design criteria. Most people don't believe that there is any hidden trapdoor in DES today.

The DES algorithm encrypts data in 64-bit blocks using a 56-bit key. Some people note that it may be almost practical to build a machine that will try all possible keys in a day. The price of this rests at about US$1 million, but the price is dropping as machines grow faster [Way92, Wie93]. For this reason, most people suggest encrypting data multiple times with different keys. A popular solution is known as *triple-DES* and it is accomplished by encrypting the data with the first key, decrypting it with a second key and encrypting it with a third. This makes the key effectively 168 bits—well outside the reach of the most powerful computers that will be developed in the foreseeable future. [1]

The basic structure of the DES algorithm is known as a *Feistel network*. Each block of 64 bits is broken into two halves with 32 bits. These are usually referred to as the left (L) and right (R) halves. The left and right halves are mixed together in 16 consecutive rounds. In each round, the left half is modified by mixing it up with the right half and then the halves are swapped. After 16 rounds, the two halves are joined back together into a 64-bit block and this is the encrypted data.

The mixing process uses a collection of *s-boxes*. This is a highly random and non-linear function that permutes the right half. The fact that it is non- linear makes it hard if not impossible to use most mathematical tools to analyze and break the encryption function. Figure 2.1 shows one of the s-boxes from DES to illustrate how they work. One test of the s-box's strength is how small changes in the input may lead to big changes in the output. Notice how one changed input bit will often lead to two or more changed output bits.

The design of the s-boxes was what the NSA and IBM classified.

Here is a step-by-step description of how each round mixes the left and right halves together. It begins with the values of the left half (L_{i-1}) and the right half (R_{i-1}) and produces new values L_i and R_i:

---

[1]Princeton researchers (Dan Boneh, Richard Lipton, and Chris Dunworth) have developed a hypothetical solution for using DNA chemistry to attack DES. The solution has not been demonstrated with actual wet chemistry but there is little doubt that it is theoretically possible. They estimate that a key could be recovered with four months of work.

$000000 \rightarrow 1110$	$000001 \rightarrow 0100$	$000010 \rightarrow 1101$	$000011 \rightarrow 0001$
$000100 \rightarrow 0010$	$000101 \rightarrow 1110$	$000110 \rightarrow 1011$	$000111 \rightarrow 1000$
$001000 \rightarrow 0011$	$001001 \rightarrow 1010$	$001010 \rightarrow 0110$	$001011 \rightarrow 1100$
$001100 \rightarrow 0101$	$001101 \rightarrow 1001$	$001110 \rightarrow 0000$	$001111 \rightarrow 0111$
$010000 \rightarrow 0000$	$010001 \rightarrow 1111$	$010010 \rightarrow 0111$	$010011 \rightarrow 0100$
$010100 \rightarrow 1110$	$010101 \rightarrow 0010$	$010110 \rightarrow 1101$	$010111 \rightarrow 0001$
$011000 \rightarrow 1010$	$011001 \rightarrow 0110$	$011010 \rightarrow 1100$	$011011 \rightarrow 1011$
$011100 \rightarrow 1001$	$011101 \rightarrow 0101$	$011110 \rightarrow 0011$	$011111 \rightarrow 1000$
$100000 \rightarrow 0100$	$100001 \rightarrow 0001$	$100010 \rightarrow 1110$	$100011 \rightarrow 1000$
$100100 \rightarrow 1101$	$100101 \rightarrow 0110$	$100110 \rightarrow 0010$	$100111 \rightarrow 1011$
$101000 \rightarrow 1111$	$101001 \rightarrow 1100$	$101010 \rightarrow 1001$	$101011 \rightarrow 0111$
$101100 \rightarrow 0011$	$101101 \rightarrow 1010$	$101110 \rightarrow 0101$	$101111 \rightarrow 0000$
$110000 \rightarrow 1111$	$110001 \rightarrow 1100$	$110010 \rightarrow 1000$	$110011 \rightarrow 0010$
$110100 \rightarrow 0100$	$110101 \rightarrow 1001$	$110110 \rightarrow 0001$	$110111 \rightarrow 0111$
$111000 \rightarrow 0101$	$111001 \rightarrow 1011$	$111010 \rightarrow 0011$	$111011 \rightarrow 1110$
$111100 \rightarrow 1010$	$111101 \rightarrow 0000$	$111110 \rightarrow 0110$	$111111 \rightarrow 1101$

Figure 2.1. This table illustrates the first DES s-box. It takes 6-bit values and spits out 4-bit ones. Note that a change in one input bit will generally change two output bits. The function is also nonlinear and difficult to approximate with linear functions.

1. L_i is easy. It is just R_{i-1}. This means that each half is really changed only eight times because each round changes only one half. The swapping also simplifies decryption. The same arrangement of s-boxes and rounds will also decrypt DES. This means that only one circuit is needed for both encryption and decryption.

2. R_{i-1} is also the beginning for R_i. R_{i-1} is expanded from 32 to 48 bits by repeating some of the bits. This is known as the *expansion permutation*. It will be represented as $EP(R_{i-1})$.

3. Then a subset of the key is chosen. These 48 bits are known as K_i.

4. The key and the expanded version of R_{i-1} are added together using the exclusive-or operation ($\oplus$).

5. There are eight s-boxes (Figure 2.1 shows the first). Each takes 6 bits and spits out 4. Together they take 48 bits and return 32 bits. If the s-boxes are represented with S, then the result after passing through the s-boxes is $S(K_i \oplus EP(R_{i-1}))$.

6. There is an additional permutation that scrambles the order of the bits again. Call this P.

7. R_i is set to be $P(S(K_i \oplus EP(R_{i-1})))$.

This set of steps makes up one round. It is repeated 16 times, producing the final result. Each half is modified by the s-boxes and mixed in with the other half eight times. The most important feature of the design is the cascading effect of a change. If you encrypt two blocks that differ by only one bit, then the end result will often be completely different. About half of the bits should be different. The mixing and countermixing ensure this.

This section has not dealt with the use of the key material. There are 56 bits in the key. Only 48 bits are used in each round. The 48 bits used in each round are different and determined by a complex permutation. After each round, the key bits are scrambled and rotated. Then a subset is chosen. This step is repeated again and again. Some people feel that the complicated permutations don't add much to the mathematical strength of the algorithm. They just make it complicated for someone to implement it in software on a general purpose machine. This is certainly true because the permutations are easy to implement in hardware but complicated in software.

The key schedule is designed with one important feature in mind. The same circuit can both encrypt and decrypt DES. So if $f_k(x)$ stands for encrypting a 64-bit string x with the key k, then $x = f_k(f_k(x))$. This feature is repeated in many of the ciphers that followed DES.

This chapter does not go into enough detail for you to implement DES on your own. There are many implementations available on the Internet. Some include `http://www.program.com/source/crypto/` and `http://www.isse.gmu.edu/ pfarrell/crypto.html`. There is also source code bound into Bruce Schneier's *Applied Cryptography*[Sch93].

Remember that most consider DES to be on the cusp of insecurity at this writing. Only 2^{55} different keys need to be checked to break DES exhaustively.[2] Most people are using triple DES, which is constructed by first encrypting with key 1, decrypting with key 2, and then encrypting with key 3.

The Differential Cryptanalysis described by Eli Biham and Adi Shamir exploits one bit changes to extract the key. But it must analyze the effects of a large number (about 2^{48}) of changes.

Other Private Key Algorithms

Some of the other private key algorithms were inspired by DES. These include Ralph Merkle's Khufu and Bruce Schneier's Blowfish. Both of

---

[2]This is because of an interesting side effect. Flipping all of the bits in the key flips all of the bits in the result. So you need to test only half of the keys to search for the answer.

these algorithms repeatedly scramble the data by mixing it up with some part of the key and an s-box. The major difference is that the mixing occurs in 8- and 32-bit blocks to increase performance on general purpose CPUs.

Another major difference is that the s-boxes are each key dependent. A standard set of s-boxes is rescrambled before encryption using the key material as a basis. This means that a new set of s-boxes is used with each key, making it impossible to use some well-known attacks. For instance, differential cryptanalysis depends upon exploiting statistical weaknesses in the s-boxes. But if you don't know the s-boxes, you can't discover these weaknesses.

RC-2 and RC-4 are two other popular algorithms developed by Ron Rivest and marketed by RSA Data Securities. They are proprietary, although someone has reverse engineered RC-4 code and posted it to the network. The ciphers use a variable amount of key. The RC-4 cipher is most popular because the U.S. government agreed to expedite export licenses for software that uses RC-4 but limits it to keys smaller than 40 bits. This does not offer very much protection.

Public Key Encryption

The most popular public key algorithm is RSA and it is widely used in many encryption systems. PGP (Pretty Good Privacy) is by far the most popular, but this is because it is free for non-commercial use. More sophisticated systems are available from Nortel and many other vendors.

The basic algorithm can be summarized very quickly, but it uses a form of arithmetic that may not be familiar to many people. The computations are all done *modulo* some number n. This system is often called "clock arithmetic" because the numbers wrap around. For instance, $2 + 3 \bmod 4 = 1$. First the two and the three are added together. If there is any amount greater than the modulo, four, then only the extra is kept. Here are some other examples: $3 \times 5 \bmod 7 = 1$, $2 + 3 \bmod 5 = 0, 5 - 6 \bmod 9 = 8$, and $3 + 7 \bmod 7 = 3$.

In effect, the only numbers that count are the values between 0 and $n - 1$. Division is a bit more complicated and it doesn't always work. If you want to understand it, you should think of division as reversing multiplication. So if you're asked to find $a/b \bmod c$, the answer will be the value d such that $d \times b \bmod c = a$. For instance, $2/3 \bmod 7 = 5$

because $2 \times 5 \mod 7 = 3$. Division is guaranteed to work only when n is prime. In other cases, it may or may not work.

The RSA algorithm "encrypts" a message by converting it into a number between 0 and $n - 1$ and then raising it to some power. The conversion can be accomplished in any number of possible ways that are beyond the scope of this book. If the message is too long to be converted into a number between 0 and $n - 1$, then it is broken up into parts and encrypted separately. The key is to think of the message as merely a number, m.

To encrypt, raise m to the power e modulo n. That is, $m^e \mod n$. For almost all e, there is a value of d that will decrypt the message: $(m^e)^d \mod n = m$. Generally, the values of e and n are published in a big directory as the public key for a person. The value of d is kept secret and secure. Anyone who wants to send a message to someone would find the personal value of e and m and compute $m^e \mod n$.

The algorithm is simple to explain and implement, but finding good values for n, e, and d can require some sophisticated work. The standard solution is to choose n to be the product of two large prime numbers p and q. The value of n is made public as part of the public key, but the values of p and q must be kept secret. No one has publicly described any good way for factoring a number n into p and q and this is the basis for the security of RSA. If someone could discover a quick and efficient method, then the algorithm would be insecure.

If you know p and q, then the value of e or d can be chosen at random. In some cases, people want d or e to be relatively small to make either decryption or encryption relatively fast. In either case, $d \times e \mod ((p - 1) \times (q - 1)) = 1$. This equation can be used to calculate e from d or vice versa using Euclid's algorithm, which is beyond the scope of this book.

Here's a quick example. Let $p = 11$ and $q = 13$, making $n = 143$. Let $e = 7$. This makes $d = 103$ because $103 \times 7 \mod 120 = 1$. If your message is 13, then $13^7 = 62748517$. Modulo 143 is 117. So 13 encrypted with the public key of 7 and 143 is 117. Notice that only values between 0 and 142 can be used and those are the only values that are returned. Only the secret key, 103, can decrypt the value: $117^{103} \mod 143 = 13$. The public key doesn't help.

This book has not described many other restrictions on the values of n, e, and d. Some values are significantly stronger than others and all of the best software packages do their best to avoid weaker keys.

Digital Signatures with RSA

Digital signatures with RSA are easy to construct. The owner of the key uses the private part, d, to sign a message by computing $m^d \mod n$

and distributing it with m. The uses of d and e are symmetric or inter-changeable. So anyone who knows e and n (everyone), can check the signature by computing $(m^d)^e \mod n$. If it equals m, then the signature is valid. Only someone who knows d could have generated it.

Digital signatures can also be constructed with hash functions alone. See page 31.

In order to save time and increase security, many digital signa-tures are not computed by encrypting the entire message, m. This message is often broken into multiple blocks and raising numbers to a power modulo n can be computationally expensive. The solution is to compute a cryptographically secure hash function, h, that boils a long message down to a short number. The digital signature be-comes $h(m)^d \mod n$ and it can be checked by anyone who can also compute h.

Hash functions are described beginning on page 30.

Maintaining Public Keys

Private key algorithms like DES are fairly straightforward to main-tain. The key must be kept secret by both parties. There are some systems, like Kerberos, that make it easier to distribute keys between people in a group, but for the most part the job involves plenty of secrecy. Trusted couriers are often used to distribute the initial key material.

Public keys systems can avoid this problem. Everyone can publish their public key information and broadcast it as widely as possible. The only danger is that there is no easy way to make sure that the public keys are authentic. For instance, an eavesdropper named Alice may want to listen in on the communication of Bob and Ray. Normally, Bob would look up Ray's key, K_{ray}, in the public directory and use it to mail a message. But if Alice could substitute her key, K_{alice}, in its place, Bob would really be encrypting the data so that only she could read it. After she received it, she would re-encrypt it with , and send it along so that Ray doesn't even know it was compromised.

One popular solution to this dilemma is the *certificate*. This is a data packet that includes the public parts of the key pair (e and n in the case of RSA) and a digital signature generated by some trusted authority. The data packet may also include extra information like your Internet address or some restrictions about the validity of the certificate.

These certificates are generated by a *certificate authority*. One of the major companies in this business right now is Verisign but many others may choose to issue certificates in the future. The certificate authority can take the necessary precautions to make sure that the matching

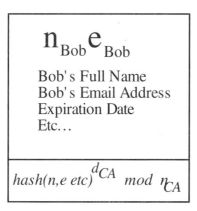

Figure 2.2. This is a visual explanation of the certificate. The data inside the box is what is guaranteed by the certificate. This is hashed into a value and then encrypted with the secret key, d_{CA}, of the certificate authority. Anyone can now trust that this is really Bob's public key because the certificate authority, CA, stands behind it.

between the person and the public key is accurate and secure. For instance, RSA Data Security offered certificates to users of MacOS who sent in a notarized document proving that a person offered the notary three forms of picture ID. Now, anyone who checks a digital signature produced by this Apple software can be sure that the match between the name and the public key was backed up by three forms of ID. This may often be enough in many cases, but some people may desire more.

Of course, anyone familiar with basic theology will recognize a potential problem here. The certificate essentially says that the certificate authority stands behind this public key. But how do you know that the certificate authority's digital signature is valid? If you wanted to check a certificate authority's signature, you could access the authority's own certificate that was guaranteed by an even higher authority.

Many users of public key encryption are planning a complex heirarchy of public key certificate authorities. At the bottom level might be a companywide certificate authority or a neighborhood authority. This would be guaranteed by a bigger company or government body, which would, in turn, also be guaranteed by an even higher body.

There must be a top to this heirarchy and this certificate will be broadly circulated so that everyone can be sure that they have an

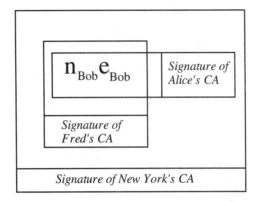

Figure 2.3. Here is a representation of multiple signatures guaranteeing a public key. The values of n_{Bob} and e_{Bob} are backed by both Fred's and Alice's certificate authorities. The entire signature is backed by New York's CA, which signed the entire package. Compare this with Figure 2.4.

accurate copy. It might be printed in newspaper advertisements and other highly public locations. It will also be built into software.

Some keys may even be guaranteed by multiple parties. A company key may be certified by both the corporate authority and the

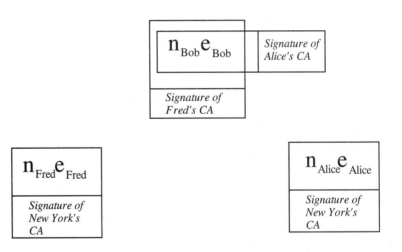

Figure 2.4. Here are three certificates. The first guarantees Bob's keys. But to check the guaranteeing signature, you need the public keys of Alice and Fred. They are provided by the certificates that are produced by New York. This is the proper structure of a hierarchical certificate system.

local government. PGP, a popular form of RSA software, does not recognize certificate authorities per se. It just allows other users to guarantee each other's key. One key, for instance, may be signed by all of the person's friends. This builds up a web of trust.

Building and maintaining these certificate authorities may prove to be one of the most important challenges of bringing commerce and accountability to the Net.

Certificates and Copyright Enforcement

All good encryption software is built to anticipate the possibility that keys will change over time. Replacing public keys every few months or a year is a good policy and the certificate authority should be designed to facilitate this use. The certificate might also contain an expiration date.

Imagine this data distribution software: A screen saver downloads new data to the screen each night and displays the news on the screen during the day. Pointcast (www.pointcast.com) already makes such a system. In order to gain market share, they distribute their screen saver software at a low price in the hope of making money by selling advertising or marketing the content later. In order to prevent others from substituting their own data stream and effectively leaching off their hard work developing the screen saver, the company decides to reprogram the screen saver to accept only authorized data. That is, every block of data must be accompanied by a valid signature.

A simple solution is to merely embed the public key of the company, K_{com}, in the software. When the company wants to distribute new data, it just uses the private half of the key pair and signs it. This would be perfectly acceptable, but it has some major limitations. First, there is no provision for changing the key if it is compromised. If hackers discover the private half of the key, then they can use all of the software available at no extra charge. If the company wants to distribute a new key, they must change all of the software.

Another problem is that the system is rigid. Anyone who wants to distribute data must have access to the private half of the key. This may be okay in small companies, but it doesn't scale well. As more people get access, the risks of compromise increase. If the company is successful getting many people to adopt the screen saver, then they may want to rent out "channels" to other data providers. This would mean revealing the secret half of the key to them.

A better solution uses certificates. The screen saver would check for a valid signature on the data. Anyone who wants to be a data provider must get a certificate that may come with an expiration date. When they create new data, they sign it using the secret half of the key and then include a copy of their certificate. The screen saver extracts the public key from the certificate and checks to see that the signature is valid.

There is still the same requirement for security of the master key used to guarantee the certificate, but the requirements are much easier to meet. The public half of the key pair is built into the software, but the secret half of the key used to sign certificates does not need to be revealed to many people. It may even be kept in a vault or secure location. Several companies even make special tamper-resistant boxes to hold this information. If a key is inadvertently compromised, new certificates can be issued.

Similar systems are already used today in electronic game systems like Nintendo or the Bandai Pippin. The company sells the hardware for a low price in the hope of making money on each game sold. The hardware checks the software before running to ensure that it contains a valid digital signature and a matching certificate.

Other Forms of Public Key Encryption

The RSA system is not the only public key encryption system available, but it is one of the best known and the most thoroughly explored. Some of the other systems, however, are notable because they can be used in different ways to help protect copyright.

The most common other system is known as *Diffie-Hellman Key Exchange* and it was named after its developers, Whitfield Diffie, and Martin Hellman. The system allows two parties to exchange messages and establish a secret key without meeting each other. This can have significant advantages and many encrypted phone systems use it to set up the key for the session.

The idea is simple and similar to RSA. Let p be a prime number. Bob chooses two random numbers, x and a, calculates $x^a \bmod p$, and then sends both x, p, and $x^a \bmod p$ to Alice. Alice chooses her own random number, b, and sends $x^b \bmod p$ back to Bob. Each of them now has enough information to calculate their shared key, $x^{ab} \bmod p$. Bob takes Alice's value, $x^b \bmod p$, and computes $(x^b)^a \bmod p$ while Alice takes Bob's number and computes $(x^a)^b \bmod p$. This value is either used as the key directly or more likely run through a hash function.

The most important question is, "Can an eavesdropper determine x^{ab} mod p?" No. There is no publicly known way to discover a from x^a mod p. This is known as the *discrete log* problem and it is hard if p is suitably large. An eavesdropper knows only x^a mod p and x^b mod p, but neither a nor b.

One major problem with Diffie-Hellman key exchange is a man-in-the-middle attack. If Charles controls the network connection between Alice and Bob, then Charles can negotiate separate keys between himself and both of them. When Alice sends a message to Bob, she really encrypts it with a key that only Charles can read and vice versa. Charles can maintain the charade as long as he decodes the message and re-encodes it fast enough to send it along without delaying it.

Encrypted telephone calls work around this problem by hashing up the agreed upon secret key and displaying it on each end. Alice would read this hash value out loud in her voice and Bob could check his display to make sure that it matches.

There is a large number of digital signature and public key encryption programs that rely upon the strength of the discrete log problem. Some consider it to be nominally safer because the RSA algorithm can be broken by either a quick way to factor or a quick way to take the discrete log. But the systems that rely upon the discrete log are not attackable if a fast factoring algorithm is discovered.

Some of these algorithms produce only digital signatures—they're not designed to hide secret information. These include the *El Gamal Signatures* designed by Tahir El Gamal and the similar *Digital Signature Algorithm* developed by the National Institute of Standards and Technology (NIST) with the likely help of the NSA. Both will produce a digital signature of the file but are not intended to hide secret messages.

The distinction is more than academic. The U.S. government actively restricts the export of software that can hide secrets. Signature-only algorithms do not fall into this definition because they're used for authentication, a lawful notion that doesn't impede surveillance.

The problem is that the algorithms are not perfect. Chapter 3 describes how these signature algorithms can carry information through a *subliminal channel* discovered by Gus Simmons. This channel can be used to customize each digital signature. If the copyrighted material is discovered in someone's possession, this personalized signature can reveal the original and lawful recipient.

Hash Functions

Hash functions were originally designed to take a wide collection of data as input and output a number between 0 and n with equal probability. This value is used to distribute the data throughout a database so it uses all of the resources effectively.

Cryptographically secure hash functions have the same mandate with tighter requirements. They take some collection of bits and reduce it to a fixed number of bits in such a way that the answers should emerge with equal probability. The additional requirement is that given a y, it should be hard to find an x such that $h(x) = y$. That is, it is hard to guess a value.

If a hash function, h, is cryptographically secure, then it can be used as a trusted surrogate for the data. Most digital signature algorithms don't do their computations on the message, m, itself. They operate on $h(m)$ which is often substantially shorter. But the cryptographically secure nature ensures that it would be difficult to find an m' such that $h(m) = h(m')$. For instance, I can't take some digital check for $100.00 and add extra zeros to make it worth $1,000,000.00 without changing the hash value for the check.

Two of the most commonly used hash algorithms are MD-5 and its cousin the Secure Hash Algorithm (SHA), which is part of the Digital Signature Standard. The SHA is based upon an earlier cousin of MD-5 known as MD-4. Both take arbitrarily long messages, but MD-5 returns a 128-bit hash value while the SHA returns 160 bits.

MD-5 operates by grabbing 512 bits of the input file, mixing it together with complicated functions, and then keeping 128 bits of the result. Then, 384 new bits are added and the process is repeated until all of the input bits are incorporated. If the input file is not the correct size, then it is padded. The SHA operates in a similar way, but it keeps 160 bits between rounds.

The core of MD-5 is four functions applied on bits:

$$F(x, y, z) = xy \ or \ (not \ x)z$$

$$G(x, y, z) = xz \ or \ y(not \ z)$$

$$H(x, y, z) = x \ xor \ y \ xorz$$

$$I(x, y, z) = y \ xor \ (x \ or \ (not \ z))$$

Normally, these functions are computed on either 16- or 32-bit blocks of the data. There is also a large amount of shifting and rotating of the bits. By the time the calculation is finished, practically every bit in the initial block has had a chance to influence the final value of every bit. This is the basis for the security. The SHA uses a similar set of functions.

The exact details of both algorithms are not important enough to include in this book, but they're available in *Applied Cryptography* [Sch93] if you're interested. Source code is also included.

Digital Signature with Hash Functions

Cryptographically secure hash functions can be used as "poor man-'s" digital signatures in some cases. For instance, many companies that distribute software over the Net will post the MD-5 value for the files. If people want to make sure that no one tampered with the files, they can compute the MD-5 value and compare it. This makes them a powerful tool for copyright holders.

More secure digital signatures can be constructed if two parties have a shared secret collection of bits, B. Let's say Alice wants to send a message, m, to Bob. She can "sign" the message by computing the hash function $h(Bm)$ by sticking B at the beginning of the message file before hashing it. When Bob receives the message, m, he can do the same thing and make sure that the values match. If they do, then only Alice could have generated the signature because only Alice knew the shared secret B.

In many situations, this type of digital signature is just as good as one produced using public key algorithms. Many digital transaction systems use such an algorithm so a customer can sign off on transactions with the bank. Both the customer and the bank can keep a shared secret so this system works.

The shared secret batch of bits, B, can be arranged by courier or negotiated using Diffie-Hellman key exchange. See page 28.

The system fails when there is no easy way to negotiate a shared secret batch of bits. If I post something on the Internet, then I want everyone to be able to check my digital signature. This will work only if I can publish half of a public key pair to the world. There is no way to publish a value B without opening up the possibility of forgery.

Time Stamping

Constructing a "time stamp" of a digital document is an intriguing question. One simple solution is to make some computer on the network act as a digital notary. If you mail it a document, it will add a time field and apply its digital signature. This can be quite useful for establishing when a document is finished. The end of creation is, in many senses, the beginning of copyright.

The one problem with this approach is that it can be forged long into the future if the notary can be corrupted. The notary could simply roll back the clock, add the old time field, and sign the document. There is no ironclad way of establishing when it really happened.

Paper-based notaries defend against this problem by keeping a notebook list of the documents they sign. They make an entry in the log for each document and if there is no entry on the proper day then the odds are good that the time of the signature is forged. This system may help, but it does nothing to prevent the document from being altered or changed outright in between.

Digital notaries have an advantage. They can enter a hash code for each document in the log. This prevents someone from substituting a new document or changing it in any way. In fact, the best solution may be to add two values to the log. Call this entry for document m_i to be H_i. The first part is the hash of the document, $h(m_i)$, and the second is the hash of this value and the previous entry, $h(m_i H_{i-1})$.

Surety Inc (www.surety.com) offers software and services for people seeking an outside source for notarizing documents. At regular times, they also print the latest entry in their hash log in advertisements in newspapers. This presents the world with an additional sense of accuracy. No one can go back and redo a log because then the hash values would not stand up.

Bit Commitment

Bit commitment algorithms are used to say "I told you so" without saying anything. They let people lock in an answer without revealing the answer to the other party. The standard example is a broker who wants to prove his ability to choose stocks without actually revealing these ideas to people who don't pay commissions.

There are two major solutions. The first is to take the secret, m, and encrypt it with a key, k. Send the answer $f_k(m)$, to the person who questions whether you know the secret. Later, after the race is over or the game is finished, you can reveal m by revealing k.

Additional security can be gained by adding an open collection of bits, B, to the front of m and shipping both B and $f_k(Bm)$ at the beginning. This B might be a string like, "Honest, I'm not lying," or it could just be another random string. This defends against the possibility that there exist some other values like $\overline{k}$ and $\overline{m}$ such that $f_{\overline{k}}(\overline{m}) = f_k(m)$. If these values exist, then a malicious person could choose between revealing either k or $\overline{k}$.

Bit commitment can also be done with cryptographically secure hash functions. Send B and $h(Bm)$ at the beginning. When it comes time to reveal the values later, send along m. The values should check out. This protocol is just as secure but it doesn't require the use of potentially unexportable encryption functions. Hash functions are generally not limited by the U.S. government because they're often considered to be usable for authentication only.[3]

Summary

Cryptography is a powerful tool for controlling the flow of information. You can:

- Use it to hide data so it is revealed only at a later date.

- Check data to make sure it is authentic.

- Force hardware or software to accept only authentic data.

- Freeze data in time so people will know that it hasn't been changed.

All of these features are ideal tools for people who hold copyrights and more information can be found later. Chapter 6 describes how data can be locked up and parceled out to people who purchase it. Chapter 3 shows how to personalize each digital signature so it can be traced.

The biggest problem with cryptography is that some governments view it as a threat to their ability to conduct surveillance. Eavesdropping on conversations can be a powerful tool against white-collar crime. The problem is that strong cryptography can also be a powerful deterrent against crime and copyright violations.

---

[3]This fact is far from the truth. Any hash function can be converted into a secret key encryption algorithm. If the key is k, then $x_1 = h(k)$, $x_2 = h(x_1)$, $x_3 = h(x_2)$ etc. These form a stream of values that can be xor'ed with the data to encrypt it. If the hash function is cryptographically secure, then this cipher should be secure as well.

The U.S. government continues to offer versions of its "Clipper" compromise. Each encryption program would be strong, but it would also include a copy of the key in a locked data packet that only the government could read. There are several different versions that include different techniques for splitting up the key. The greatest danger is that the key recovery center would disclose the key through a mistake, a bribe, or after espionage. Some consider this threat minor and others consider it dangerous enough to make these key recovery schemes unworkable.

These export restrictions should prove to be especially onerous to copyright holders. The creative talents in the United States are a major source of revenues. The film and television industries dominate the world and bring in a fortune to the United States. Copyright infringement is the greatest threat to this revenue stream. The United States and China are constantly bickering over the terms of the treaties and whether China is doing enough to combat copyright infringement. Many other countries are just as lax.

Encryption software may be a good technique for controlling copyright problems in America, but there is little reason to believe that foreign countries will be interested in cryptographic solutions that give the U.S. government an open invitation to read their documents. Why should they invest in this insecure solution?

There may be compromises available to specific information providers. A particular data delivery service may produce specialized software that will decrypt the data for legitimate recipients. The government may also be a customer or the company may provide access to the data stream gratis. If the software is not usable to keep arbitrary secrets from the government, then it may be easy to get an export license.

Chapter 3

Subliminal Signatures

Subliminal channels in digital signature algorithms are often over-looked, but they can offer copyright holders a unique method for con-trolling their product. They can send extra data through the signature that can't be removed.

Sending Messages through Signatures

Subliminal channels are an excellent tool for copyright protection be-cause they provide a way to add a piggyback message to a digital sig-nature without interfering with the operation of the signature. They are best used in a situation in which some software wants to check a digital signature before displaying the information. If the signature is not valid, the software will assume the data is not accurate.

A subliminal signature makes it possible to add some identification or tagging bits to each copy without interfering with the operation of the digital signature software. Each copy of the document will look the same and each signature will be different, but anyone checking the signatures will find they are all valid.

Gus Simmons developed the science of subliminal channels while working at Sandia National Labs [Sim84, Sim85, Sim86]. These chan-nels act like hidden cubbyholes in a particular algorithm where ad-ditional information can be stored away. Most basic algorithms like DES have no known subliminal channel. They are usually found

in digital signature algorithms like the Digital Signature Standard
(DSS)[Smi93, NIS91] and its predecessor, the system developed by
Taher El Gamal [ElG85].

Subliminal channels are available whenever the function that converts the data into the signature is not one-to-one. That is, for every
value of x, there may be several values of $f(x)$ that could be generated. They all must be valid, which is to say that $f^{-1}(f(x)) = x$. Basic
encryption methods like one-time pads and simple ciphers are all one-
to-one so there is no subliminal channel. Ciphers like DES cannot have
subliminal channels because the size of their input is equal to the size
of their output. DES takes in 64 bits and spits out 64 encrypted bits. If
there was some subliminal channel, then there would be multiple possible values for each code word. A simple counting argument shows
how this isn't possible.

Subliminal channels are often found in digital signature algorithms
because the process of crippling the public key encryption often leaves
the secondary channel available for holding a message. Signature-only
schemes are often used in political situations where authentication is
necessary but secrets are forbidden. The U.S. government prevents the
export of encryption software that maintains secrets, but it places little
restriction on software that can be used only to prove authenticity.

The most basic subliminal channel can be found in the El Gamal
signature system. The subliminal channels are not a problem for this
system, but they are not particularly elegant. Both parties must know
the secret key in the El Gamal system before they can exchange data.
This removes much of the advantages of using a public key system.

El Gamal Encryption

The El Gamal system [ElG85] begins with a large prime number, p, and
two random numbers g and r. From this, it is possible to compute:

$$q = g^r \bmod p.$$

The values of p, q, and g are distributed publicly as the user's public
key. In many cases, the values of p and g are fixed because they can be
reused without affecting the security of the algorithm. The value of r
is the private key and it must be protected because it is necessary for
generating a signature, or for adding a subliminal channel.

The basic El Gamal system uses a random number to choose among the possible signatures. Call this k. If a subliminal message is being sent, it can be used in place of k because the value of k can be recovered if you know r. This value of k must be relatively prime to $p - 1$. Let $a = g^k \bmod p$.

Let the value being signed be m. This is probably the result of hashing the message because m must be smaller than p. Find b by solving this equation:

$$m = ra + kb \bmod p - 1.$$

The Euclidean algorithm used to find the least common divisor can be reversed to find the multiplicative inverse if you know r and k. Neither of these values can be revealed without compromising the signature.

The two values, a and b, act as the signature and can be checked by computing:

$$y^a a^b \bmod p = g^m \bmod p.$$

If the two values are equal, then the signature matches. You can think of the process as finding a line that goes through some points.

If k holds a subliminal message instead of a random number, then it can be recovered from the values of a and b:

$$bk = m - ra \bmod p - 1.$$

A subliminal message like this requires knowing r to recover the message. The advantage of this is that random users will not be able to recover the tagging bits even if they have several signatures of the same document. This prevents people from forging the tags on a document.

The disadvantage is that the value of r may need to be revealed to the court or some neutral body to prove the existence of the tagging bits. This would reveal the public key and allow anyone to forge signatures in the future. If such a system was used widely, then it would make plenty of sense to have a system for changing keys.

Another tagging system can also be produced through the inefficient process of random selection. If you want to tag a document with value u from tags between 0 and $v - 1$, then keep choosing random values of k until either a or b modulo v is equal to u. Clearly, this grows more and more inefficient as v gets large. Still, this approach does not require revealing the value of r.

The Federal Standard, DSS, and Subliminal Channels

The algorithm is known as Digital Signature Algorithm (DSA), but its recognition as the standard also makes it the Digital Signature Standard (DSS).

The federal government through the National Institute of Standards and Technology (NIST) recognized a signature-only algorithm for use by federal agencies moving non-classified information around the world. This algorithm, which produces 160-bit signatures, was designed with the assistance of the NSA.

The DSS is also capable of carrying subliminal data because it operates in a fashion similar to the El Gamal signature scheme. Several changes, however, make it possible to ship data without revealing the secret key—a serious advantage in the world of copyright protection. Many people can decode the tagging data without knowing the secret key that generated the signature. This may be useful if you want individual computers to make decisions about displaying data by reading the tagging bits. For instance, one bit may say "Display this data only to adults" so the algorithm could be used in parental control technology.

The DSA also begins with a prime number, p, that may be used by several people or groups. The size of this may range between 512 and 1024 bits. The standard insists that the size be a number of bits that satisfies this equation: $512 + 64i$, where i is an integer.

The big difference between the DSA and the El Gamal signature system is that there is also a value, q, that must be a 160-bit prime factor of $p - 1$. This extra requirement makes it somewhat harder to generate the secret keys. The easiest solution is to begin with q and multiply it by some random value, z, until $rz + 1$ is prime.

There is also a value of g, which unlike the El Gamal scheme is not random. It is based upon h, some number where $h^k \bmod p$ is not one nor zero when $k = \frac{p-1}{q}$. Let $g = h^k$.

This value of g is used to select a random value, x, and compute $y = g^x \bmod p$. The value of x is the private key, but y is distributed with the public key. $p, q,$ and g are also part of the public key, but they may be shared by a group at some cost to the security of the system.

The signature is constructed by choosing a random number, k, as before and producing two values: $r = (g^k \bmod p) \bmod q$ and $s = (k^{-1}(H(m) + xr)) \bmod q$. These two values act as the signature and both are about 160 bits long. The function $H(m)$ is a special hash function also specified by the federal government known as the Secure Hash Algorithm. It is quite similar to MD-5. m is the message being signed.

Verifying the signature is not as easy as it is with the El Gamal algorithm. It takes four calculations:

$$w = s^{-1} \ mod \ q$$

$$u_1 = (H(m) \times w) \ mod \ q$$

$$u_2 = (r \times w) \ mod \ q$$

$$v = ((g^{u_1} \times y^{u_2}) \ mod \ p) \ mod \ q$$

The value of v must equal the value of r for the signature to be valid. NIST offered a proof that the mathematics work out, but the reader should be able to generate the same [NIS91, NIS94, Smi93].

A subliminal message can be passed along through the choice of k. If the recipient knows the secret key, x, then the value of k can be recovered by inverting the equations that generated r and s. This message can be up to 160 bits long.

The same technique of choosing random values of k until r or s turns out to have a particular modulus can also be used here. This solution, however, can be monitored by anyone who knows that it is going on. The values of r or s can be watched. Simmons extends this by sending the information as the *quadratic residue* of r.

Given some random prime number, u_1, the value of r is said to be a quadratic residue mod u_1 if there exists a square root of r. That is, there exists some value a such that $a^2 \ mod \ u_1 = r$. A value of r can be checked to see if it is a quadratic residue by computing the Jacobi symbol. See Schneier [Sch94] for source code in C to accomplish this.

Simmons sends one bit of a message by choosing k until r either has or has no square root. If the bit is 1, then he chooses k until r is a right quadratic residue mod u_1. Otherwise, he keeps choosing k until r is not a quadratic residue. The odds of being finding the right value of k are exactly 50/50 if u_1 is prime.

More bits of information can be sent by choosing more prime values. If n bits are to travel down the subliminal channel, then n primes, $\{u_1, \ldots, u_n\}$, are chosen. The odds of finding the right value of k get longer and are proportional to 2^n.

This subliminal scheme does not require revealing the secret key, x, to recipients. They must know the prime numbers $\{u_1, \ldots, u_n\}$, but someone who doesn't know the prime numbers can't determine if a message is being sent.

Summary

Most digital signature schemes can carry information in a subliminal channel and this data can be used to tag a document without interfering with the signature verification process.

Of course, another tagging algorithm can also be used independently of any digital signature scheme. The data might be tagged with one of the other algorithms presented here or it might even include a separate field with the tagging data in the clear. This also would not interfere with the verification of the signature without the computations of trying to exploit a subliminal channel.

The main advantage of the subliminal channel is that its use can't be detected. If people don't know the hidden prime numbers, then they can't recover the secret bits in the subliminal channel. There is no way to be certain that the value of k was chosen randomly.

One of the biggest problems may be establishing a certificate infrastructure for non-RSA signatures. The company and the algorithm it essentially controls are market leaders and other signature algorithms with subliminal channels may not be as easily integrated into the certificate heirarchy. Any content distributor, however, may choose to use the technology on a private basis and not rely on any relatively public infrastructure.

Chapter 4

Compression

Compression algorithms are a well-known part of computer science. But they are also a good tool for marking documents because they are tuned to identifying patterns in the data. This makes them ideal tools for fiddling with the patterns in an unobtrusive way.

Writer v. Editors

Whereas a recent study published in the *Journal of the American Medical Association* establishes a link between a person's prose style and the occurrence of Alzheimer's disease and shows that people who write grammatically simple sentences often succumb much earlier than those who share their vision of life's rich pageant with the world through their words and the fully embroidered fabric of their expansive sentences.

Plaintiff contends that the defendants, his editors, have deliberately conspired with malice aforethought to limit the complexity of his prose, thus encouraging an early beginning of Alzheimer's disease in the name of boosting their corporation's profits by providing the reader/customer with a salient point presented in crisp, clear, and simple sentences.

Plaintiff contends that the defendants cravenly and insistently encouraged the plaintiff to surrender to the shackles of simplicity instead of raging, raging against the dying of the light by returning his manuscripts with discouraging comments demanding that he "get to the point", "stop using such insanely convoluted logic", "write an introduction not a treatise", "forget about a joint Nobel Prize in Physics and Literature", and "just give the readers something simple they can talk about at the watercooler now that football is over".

Plaintiff offers as further evidence his carefully constructed and artfully illustrated notes from a remedial course on "Writing with Efficiency" that he was forced to attend by the management in the hope of driving out the great Ziegfeld Follies of creativity that dances daily in his head presenting a wildly diverse (but very entertaining) collection of gamin ice dancers that inspire him to join his paragraphs with smooth transitions; tap dancing, tuxedo-clad elephants that remind him of the importance of the rhythm of prose; and blindfolded kick-boxers who demonstrate that plenty of whirling and grunting can make the impact much more exciting.

Plaintiff respectfully contends that such enforced simplicity rendered him immune to the siren calls of his muse and the delightful and witty insights she offered to him as she flitted and fluttered around the region of his soul responsible for introspection and self-conscious deliberation of the terminal condition of man. More important, the shackles of simplicity dulled his ability to feel the relentless tragedy of extinction, the prospects for a true and lasting peace that envelops the world with its blessing, the hope for a simple solution to the raging tides of pollution, and the conundrum of whether the designated hitter rule is a net win for baseball, if one can use the word "net" to describe a sport played without a net.

Plaintiff further contends that his editor-inflicted deafness to the song of his muse forced his brain to see the world through a very simple model that assumed that there was either a definite, provable causal link between two actions or there was just "nothing worth printing", thereby shutting his mind's eye to the wonderful gray clouds of nuance that blow across the plains of our mind in roiling, thundering storms of thought rearranging the landscape of knowledge through the force of the wind of intuition and the unstoppable urgency of the water of reality seeking the ocean of truth.

Plaintiff argues that the efforts of his editors to limit his sentence complexity qualify as a bona fide conspiracy prosecutable under the RICO act for treble damages because the editors were all members of the American Society of Editors and Stylemasters, an organization whose motto, "Tell the truth simply", reveals a deliberate effort to corral the American mind, break its wandering, curious spirit, and sentence it to a life of blank-eyed ignorance chewing and rechewing a cud of facts, just the facts, ma'am.

Plaintiff requests damages of $10 million to be trebled by the RICO provisions to $30 million in order to compensate him for the loss at the rate of $1 per occurrence for 10 million instances of neat simile, subtle nuance, wanton braggadocio, learned allusion, cool metaphor, blithe elision, deep thought, witty juxtaposition, and elegantly insightful profundity that will be missing from his future life as the disease dims the mortal luminescent coil in the bulb burning in the creative office of his heart.

Plaintiff acknowledges that this is just an estimate, but he has drastically reduced his request to compensate for the pleasure of knowing that the disease will strike his simpleminded editors long before it brings him down.

Compressing Data

Compression is the art and science of taking some data and representing it with a smaller number of bits. For the most part, the algorithms are fairly sophisticated schemes for finding and creating abbreviations and shorthand for the most common patterns in the data. They take the baroque and the rococo and boil it down by identifying the redundant parts.

The U.S. Postal Service, for instance, has two-letter abbreviations for the states because these names are common in addresses. Chemists have their own abbreviations for elements. Compression algorithms analyze a file and determine the most common patterns that can be replaced efficiently.

Most copyright holders that distribute their data electronically understand that compressing their data can save money by reducing the need for more disks or network bandwidth. The algorithms are quite common in many layers of the software world and many users may not even be aware that compression and decompression are taking place. This book does not focus on the common use for the algorithms in part because there are long books that already focus on the subject. (See, for instance, James Storer's bookw [Sto88].)

Compression algorithms, however, are also useful tools for defending copyrighted data by including personalized tags inside the data. The algorithms are finely tuned to spot patterns in data and this facility can be exploited in several different ways. The simplest approach uses compression algorithms to reveal the major patterns in the data so that information can be hidden in the minor patterns or the noise. This type of solution works well with images and compression functions like JPEG or MPEG.

Chapter 11 describes how to model data with waves either for compression or to add tags.

Another straightforward approach is to hide the tagging information inside some of the compression algorithm's ancillary data. A compression algorithm will often create a dictionary or a statistical model of the data that must be available to decompress the data. This usually travels with the data. The structure of this model can be permuted, in many cases, to hide information without affecting the underlying data.

The final use of compression technology is more subtle. If compression algorithms detect patterns and use them to introduce abbreviations, then what happens when they are run in reverse with random data? The result can mimic the original data. This can effectively hide the information from a tag by making it look like the original thing. The tag exists alongside in disguise.

These three solutions can be used in different combinations with different compression algorithms. Not all algorithms work well with each approach and some may not be good solutions for any of them. This chapter will discuss several basic compression algorithms and then describe how they can be adapted to carry hidden information. Many of the techniques can be extended to other compression algorithms and the details are left to the readers.

Huffman Coding

Huffman compression is one of the simplest techniques available and it has been well known and exploited since it was developed in the 1950s. The algorithm is built upon one simple observation: variable length codes can save space if the short codes are assigned to the most common patterns or characters. The Morse code used over radio and telegraphs is a good example. Letters that are common in English get a short representation (e=·, t=−) while less common letters get long representations (p=· − −·).

The Huffman algorithm identifies the most common letters in a file and then automatically assigns variable length codes to them in order to minimize the final size of the file. The codes are all variable length strings of ones and zeros that have one distinguishing feature: no code for one letter is a prefix for another letter's code. This principle makes it possible to decode the file. For instance, if A gets the code 01, B is assigned 10, and C becomes 0110, then it would be impossible do decode a file that began with the bits 0110. It could be either AB or C. The fact that the code for A is a prefix for the code for C screws everything up.

The algorithm for assembling a Huffman code does an elegant job of assigning the codes without violating this principle. The solution is surprisingly simple and uses a basic data structure known as the tree.

(Here's a short paragraph of explanation for readers unschooled in the shorthand terminology used by computer scientists to describe data structures known as trees. A *tree* consists of *nodes* containing data and *branches* that join the nodes together. One node is normally considered to be the *root*. All nodes that are directly connected to it by branches are considered to be *descendants* or *children*. These nodes may have their own descendants or children. If they do, then they are often called *interior nodes*. If they don't, then they are called *leaves*. Figure 4.1 shows a basic *binary* tree which has two branches at each interior

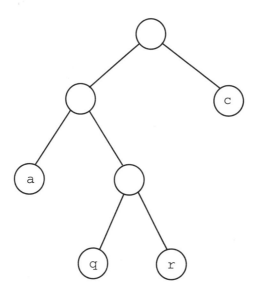

Figure 4.1. A basic tree used to hold data. This version is binary because it has two branches at each interior node. The leaves have no branches, but in this example they are the only ones that hold any data.

node. The root is at the top and the leaves contain letters. The trees are usually drawn with their root at the top because most algorithms that analyze trees start at the top.)

The Huffman algorithm constructs a binary tree and places each character from the file in a different leaf. The variable length code is determined by creating an address for each leaf by following the path from the root to the leaf. The tree is binary, so each interior node has two branches leaving it. If one branch is labeled 0 and the other is labeled 1, then the path from root to leaf can be represented by a string of zeros and ones. This path satisfies the prefix requirement.

Figure 4.2 shows a simple tree for several characters. The path from the root to the character "a" follows the edges labeled 0 and 0 so the compressed version of "a" is "00". The compressed version of "s" is "010" and "t" is "011". A full-sized tree compressing a file may have 256 leaves for each of the 256 possible bytes of data. Or, if the file is text, it might have about 30,000 leaves containing each of the standard words from English. There are many variations for how the file is chopped up into characters, but these are the most common.

The algorithm for creating the tree is simple. Count the occurrence of the n characters in the file and build n trees each containing one node that is both the root and the sole leaf of that tree. Record the character and the character count in the leaf. This count is also the

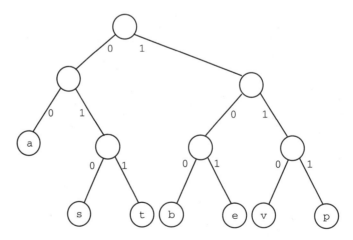

Figure 4.2. A small Huffman tree constructed for a small collection of characters. The final code for each character is the path between the root and the leaf.

count for all characters in the tree. Then repeat this loop until there is only one tree:

1. Find the two trees with smallest count for all of the characters in their leaves. At the beginning, this will be the two one-leaf trees with the least common characters.
2. Create a new node and two branches that point to the root of both of these trees. This joins the two trees and makes them one.
3. Add up the count of characters for the two trees and make this the total for the new tree.

When this algorithm is complete, there will be one tree with one root and one path to each character. The most common characters which have the greatest count will appear on leaves that are closest to the root. This means they will have shorter paths and shorter strings of zeros and ones that represent them.

Although the construction of the tree does not make it apparent, the final tree is the best possible tree for compressing the file. If all of the characters from the original file are replaced with their Huffman codes, then the final size will be the smallest possible using Huffman compression. This size is like a weighted average of the length of the codes. The most common characters are replaced by shorter codes and the least common with longer ones. The final result is the best possible solution. The proof of this fact is beyond the scope of this book, but it revolves around the fact that swapping any two leaves will increase the final size of the file.

The Huffman tree algorithm is used again and again in many different contexts. The basic approach of using each of the 256 possible bytes as the characters in the tree will often yield a respectable amount of compression. But other algorithms that are able to recognize multiple character patterns often do better. They can identify longer phrases like "with all due respect" and replace them with shorter codes. Often, a preliminary stage of analysis identifies all of the major phrases and then Huffman coding is used to assign them binary codes.

Using Huffman Coding for Tags

The Huffman coding algorithm offers a good place to hide information. The final tree or table of codes assigned each character must be

[Way88] shows a simple, easy-to-break cipher that uses this permutation notion to remove repetition in compressed files.

available before the file can be uncompressed. The structure of this table has plenty of room for manipulation and it can be easily personalized. Each person can get a different tree and the structure of the tree could be used to identify the person.

Figure 4.3 shows another version of the tree in Figure 4.2. The leaves are all at the same levels, but the paths are different. This means the codes are different, but they have the same length. The final compressed file will still have the same length if either tree is used. The tree was permuted by swapping the left and right descendants of some of the nodes.

There are many arbitrary schemes for scrambling the Huffman tree. All of them are equivalent and any tagging scheme may simply want to record the order of the letters on the tree. The simplest way to do this is to make a list of lists. The first list contains the letters on the first level from left to right. The second list contains the letters on the second level, etc. The tree from Figure 4.3 would be recorded {*}, {*,*}, {*,a,*,*}, {s,t,e,v,b,p}. The asterisks stand for empty slots.

The trees can be scrambled by simply scrambling the letters and asterisks at each level. {*}, {*,*}, {*,*,*,a}, {s,v,e,t,p,b} is another version. If the letters are scrambled on each level, then they will maintain the same distance from the root and the overall compression ratio will be unchanged.

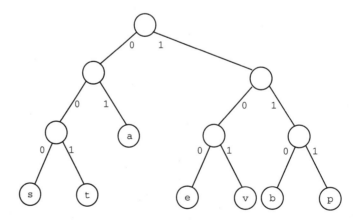

Figure 4.3. This figure shows a different version of the tree in Figure 4.2. The codes for each character are different, but the lengths are the same. The final size of any file compressed with this tree will be the same.

Standard Compression Algorithms

The great advantage of this scheme is that the tagged data can be distributed and unpacked by off-the-shelf software. If a company creates a tagged archive, they don't need to distribute a special decompression package to install it. They may want to do this for other reasons, but they are not required to do it. Any Huffman decompression algorithm could unpack it.

Many standard packages try several compression algorithms before settling on one. Most of the other algorithms can be modified in a similar way.

Using Huffman Codes for Mimicry

The Huffman compression algorithm also makes a good tool for mimicking the structure of data. If a file of random data is decompressed with a particular tree, then the characters that come out will have the same statistical structure as the file that produced the tree. For instance, let $c_A(B)$ stand for the process of compressing file B using the tree constructed from the character counts of the letters in file A. Normally, a user would use $c_A(A)$ to compress a file.

Let $c_A^{-1}(B)$ stand for the process of decompressing a file B using the statistical distribution of characters in A. If the values of 0 and 1 are randomly distributed throughout B, then the output of this decompression should have the same statistical profile as file A. That is, the characters that are common in A should also be common in $c_A^{-1}(B)$. Naturally, $c_A^{-1}(c_A(B))$ should be equal to B.

Similar studies of producing statistically equivalent text were called Travesties. See [KO84].

Here's a sample of some mimicry data that was set up to mimic the statistical profile of this chapter using different orders of statistics. First order statistics determine the chances that a letter will occur in the text. Second order statistics determine the odds that a letter will follow each particular letter. A separate table must be generated for each possible letter. This makes the process more complicated, but also more accurate. The letter t is often followed by an h, but rarely by a q.

Third order statistics examine each pair of letters and determine the odds of another letter following them. A th is often followed by a vowel in English, but rarely by another consonant. Fourth order statistics look at the odds of letters following a triplet of letters, etc.

Greater order statistics offer greater verisimilitude for text. The structure of most languages using the roman alphabet is highly redundant. Many combinations of letters occur frequently with each other. Here are five samples constructed by analyzing the statistics of letters in an early draft of this chapter. It should be obvious that the ability to mimic the result increases with more detailed statistics.

Order 3 the aptions wite ingthe roach stan the ot thms. The hareffmal of a sont, band th. The re thms and be posigureence. The dese. In to isystree com compretc. The orend ustain ass inence, tre res. If compreeduce comprefter re. The pactinstione. algorithidd pa-timags codepaccus coeffing to thics astion bette or eat to binge scrition tooluessideractications mic theirs itheiree res th

Order 4 Crease noisy on in dete for must coefficients how to high frequent each of of then can be ext will data. This instanchem Cre-ating up instart andant if the infor each including system the that addition addition a differe is decontain orithough they a station image. For trees. Figure will be eith of count be data bit patters will of in lents ther tree short can compresult it consistructers are ones for in of the or the copyright. Service, but oth informations for in abbreviation path each use is mode finality can and up the stating a smally has permtree can can in thered any compressed it withm is and be hight-for MPEG

Order 5 The Huffman algorithms world and for a smaller ones for each characters on is label huffman Coding up.

The about 2 bits the trees. Chapter is surprising it might-forward the odds of they dont, the codes to add up introducing the new node for a statistically common letterns informations when accu-racy. It shows a difference of using ther. The paths and it with the ingth collectronicallest approach personalized. Each get a dic-tion of the com connected to letter will be node a spectable. The coefficience abbreviations and detect patter pixel. {*,*}, {*}, {*}, {*}, {*}, {*}, {s,t,e,v,b,p}. This can be eithere are is books the stand the compression of exploited scients

Statistics and Tree Size

More detailed statistics, however, are often not better at hiding data. A first order Huffman tree constructed for a text file may include leaves for about 60 characters (52 letters and punctuation). The paths may be relatively long and several bits of information can be hidden, on average, for each character.

A second order Huffman tree may also have 60 characters, but it will probably have much less. Some letters like q are followed only by a u, while some letters are followed only by a small subset. Separate Huffman trees must be constructed for each letter based upon the odds of another letter following it. The letters with few followers will have small trees with short paths and codes. They will hide less bits per character. In the case of q, there will be only one node and there will be no way to hide information.

The number of bits hidden per character will generally decline as the order increases. The quality of mimicry will increase, but the cost will be paid in less data.

Quality of Mimicry

The process of mimicry can be used to hide data effectively by letting some tagging information assume the statistical "look" of other data. The value of this, of course, is limited by the context and the chance that someone or something will be able to determine that the data is fake. For instance, a weather report for southern California will often use numbers in the 70s to describe the temperature in Fahrenheit. If these values are used as the statistical model for generating a fake weather report, then the results will be believable. The secret code 007 might be sent with the sentence, "The temperature will be 70 in Burbank, 70 in downtown LA and 77 in Anaheim today."

But elementary school arithmetic lessons also include numbers, but they must make sense. If the order of the numbers is chosen to hide information, then the results may not add up. For instance, 3, 7 and 2 are numbers, but if they are chosen to hide information and placed in a sentence, then the sentence "3 + 7 = 2" may not add up.

JPEG

The JPEG algorithm was developed by the Joint Photographic Experts Group during the 1980s and it is now one of the mostopular ways to compress still images. A similar system for moving images (MPEG) is also quite common. Both algorithms are built on top of the *discrete cosine transform* (DCT), an algorithm that finds a set of coefficients that allow a small set of cosine functions to approximate a portion of the image. These coefficients take much less space to store.

A good source for complete information on JPEG is the book by K. R. Rao and J. J. Hwang. [RH96]

The JPEG standard is fairly flexible because it can operate at many different levels of accuracy. It is most efficient when it is allowed to lose information during compression and uncompression. That is, the final image is not the same as the starting image, but it comes close. In this mode, the algorithm may take only about 0.25 bit to represent each pixel.

The relationship between accuracy and compressed file size is fairly understandable. Larger compressed files do a better job of reproducing the original file when they are uncompressed. Files that take about 1 bit per pixel are usually quite excellent and the pictures are often indistinguishable when about 2 bits per pixel are used. There is also a mode in the standard that guarantees lossless recovery of the initial image, but it is not used that often.

There are two major uses for the JPEG compression standard. The first is to identify the noisy or inconsequential corners of an image. Compressing and uncompressing an image will produce a simpler approximation of the image that can be compared with the original to find noisy pixels. A solution like those in Chapter 9 that stores information in the pixels can use this information and store more data in the noisy pixels without worrying about disturbing the image.

The second solution is to actually hide information in the compressed data. The JPEG algorithm can also tolerate minor changes in the coefficients produced by the DCT. If these are modulated slightly, then they can carry information in the choices. Chapter 9 describes how to modulate the values of the pixels to carry information. This process just takes place at a higher level after the compression occurs.

Both of these solutions are important tools for anyone designing an algorithm for protecting copyright by tagging the data.

The Discrete Cosine Transform

The heart of the JPEG algorithm is the discrete cosine transform that finds a small number of coefficients for some cosine functions that can do a good job approximating a section of the image. The JPEG algorithm uses 8×8 blocks of pixels and fits them with a set of cosine functions. The luminance and chromanence (from the YCbCr) are compressed separately and the algorithm assumes that 8 bits of accuracy are used to represent each color independently.

The 8×8 block of pixels is modeled with a collection of discrete representations of a two-dimensional set of cosine functions. There are

64 possible discrete representations of these cosine functions labeled $C^{(u,v)}$ where both u and v range between 0 and 7. Each of these discrete representations is itself an 8×8 block of cosine values. The i, j entry of the model $C^{(u,v)}$ is:

$$C_{i,j}^{(u,v)} = \cos\left[\frac{\pi}{16}(2i + 1)u\right] \cos\left[\frac{\pi}{16}(2j + 1)v\right].$$

This is illustrated in Figure 4.4, which does a better job of showing the intensities as a density plot.

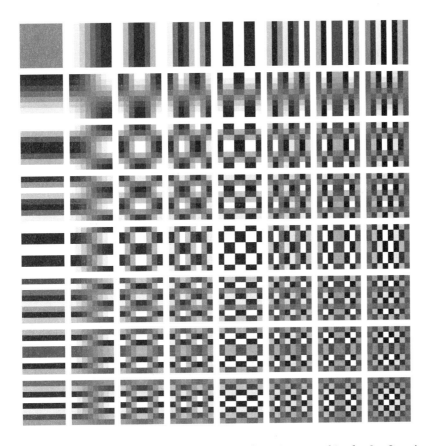

Figure 4.4. Here are the 64 different discrete functions used in the 8×8 cosine transform to model a block of 8×8 pixels in the JPEG algorithm.

The discrete cosine transform finds a different coefficient for each function so that the weighted sum of the functions adds up to recreate the original 8×8 block of pixels. That is, it finds $a_{u,v}$ so that:

$$\sum_{s=0}^{7}\sum_{t=0}^{7} a_{s,t} C^{(s,t)}$$

is the same as the original 8×8 block of pixels. The algorithm is beyond the scope of this book, but it is discussed in detail in [RH96] by K. R. Rao and J. J. Hwang.

Taking the DCT to JPEG

The DCT produces a set of coefficients for each 8×8 block of pixels. These coefficients, however, are not the final data stored in the file. The JPEG committee recognized that many of the coefficients often take some values more often than others. The algorithm saves additional space by using a Huffman coding system to save the coefficients. The most common coefficients are represented with short bit strings and the least common ones with long bit strings.

The process for converting the DCT coefficients into their final values is fairly arcane. The committee added many extra layers and small tweaks to optimize the compression at the cost of making the description rather complicated. The DCT coefficients are "quantized", which effectively removes the smallest ones from consideration. Blocks of pixels with relatively constant values will have only a few low-frequency coefficients at the end and these blocks will show great compression. Parts of the image which change rapidly or include many noisy details will include substantial higher-frequency coefficients as well. These increase the size of the compressed data describing the particular 8×8 block.

The tradeoff between the amount of compression and the quality of the final uncompressed image occurs at this point. If a large amount of compression is desired, then the high-frequency coefficients from the DCT are left out. The resulting image is flatter and more constant because the high-frequency information is left out. If the goal is a better final image, then the high-frequency terms are included at the cost of a larger compressed file.

The compressed JPEG file does not store the actual coefficients for each 8×8 block. It only stores the difference between this block and

the previous block. This difference can often be quite small. The JSteg
system developed by Derek Upham stores information by replacing
the least significant bit of this difference with the hidden data.

Using JPEG to Identify Noise

The algorithms developed in Chapter 9 describe how to hide one or
more bits in a pixel by replacing the least significant bits with the
new data. The algorithms that take this approach generally choose
a standard number of bits to use for each pixel. This has the advantage of being standard, but it can be less efficient. Replacing the least
significant bit will yield only one eighth of a standard file.

   More data can be stored without disturbing the images if the noisy
sections can be found. Changing a pixel's intensity can make a significant impact if the pixel is in the middle of a smooth, homogeneous
region of the image, but the impact is much smaller in noisy segments.
The JPEG algorithm identifies the noisy sections of the image when it
compresses an image. When the algorithm is set at high compression,
the high-frequency components of each block are ignored.

   If I is an image and $JPEG(I)$ is the compressed version of the image, then the differences between I and $JPEG^{-1}(JPEG(I))$ illuminate the
noisy segments of the image. These noisy segments are prime places
to include information by changing the least significant bits. In many
of these regions, it may be possible to flip multiple bits without degrading the quality of the image. If one pixel has value 10010100 in
the original and 10011000 in the image after JPEG compression and
decompression, then the three least significant bits are fair game. The
JPEG algorithm decided that the pixel could withstand a change of 5
units of change. Less aggressive changes may tweak only the two least
significant bits.

Summary

The chapter examined compression algorithms from a different angle
than traditional texts. While contentmongers will always have a need
for compression, this chapter concentrated on the way that compression algorithms analyze data, identify patterns, and strip away the
extra detail to produce a leaner package.

   Pattern identification can be used in copyright protection in three
ways. First, the extra data structures used for holding the decom-

pression information can be adjusted to store unique tags; second, the compression algorithms can be inverted to produce statistically similar text; and third, the compression algorithms can also identify areas that are noisy and able to sustain plenty of subtle modification to encode information.

There is no reason why many other compression schemes can't be adapted to the job of including hidden tags. Paul Davern and Michael Scott show how to adapt some of the common fractal compression schemes. [DS96]

This chapter has not addressed all of the other compression algorithms in common usage. The approaches in this chapter can be extended to other algorithms if it is possible to identify how the other algorithms find patterns.

Chapter 5

Codes and Errors

Data must be represented in some format. This chapter describes several more robust formats like error-correcting codes that can be quite useful in marking documents. Error-correcting codes help make the documents more resistant to tampering.

Bad Code in the Node

The setting is a shady pharmacy in the middle of summer. The customer has a bad cold and repeated coughs and wheezes.

Customer: I have a code.
Pharmacy: Say no more. Wink-wink!
C: Nohb. I can't speak.
P: I understand. Say no more. Wink, Wink!
C: My nossse.
P: I see. We have some very good Colombian solutions. Very popular in Bogotá, if you know what I mean.
C: Nohb.
P: Colombia. South America. Land of the coca plant. And I don't mean Coca-Cola manufacturing plant.
C: Nohb. I don't want Coke.
P: Say no more. So is this part of the code as well? Is your stopped up, nasal "Nohb" really mean "Yes?"

C: Nohb!

P: Say no more! Now, I can get you any amount? Would ten grams be enough?

C: Nohb!

P: I must say that this is a very annoying code. Now, would you like me to convert it to crack? We do it as a service.

C: Nohb!

General Codes

Chapter 2 describes how to encrypt data so it can be securely hidden from people without the proper keys. Another common word for this is a "code". The word, however, has a more general meaning that includes all possible ways of representing information in a different form. This chapter will describe several different ways of representing information that are commonly known as codes. They don't offer much security from a person because there is no key, per se, but they can be important tools for copyright protection.

Different codes are useful for defending the copyright of some data because they can be used to embed tags in the data. These tags may identify the owner, the copyright holder, or the person or organization with a rightful license to use the data. The codes can make the tags harder to read and more resistant to errors. They can also be the basis for elementary tagging.

The study of codes is a broad and deep branch of applied mathematics. This book cannot begin to do justice to the wide variety of codes and the situations in which they may be applicable. These next sections introduce basic concepts that may be useful in simple schemes of copyright defense, but more complicated and sophisticated approaches will require deeper study. Benjamin Arazi offers a good basic treatment of error-correcting codes in [Ara88]. Other good explorations of the topics include James Storer's book on data compression [Sto88].

Error-Correcting Codes

Error-correcting codes allow a computer to recover data if one or more of the bits in the file are changed. They are widely used in all parts of the machine to clean up the mistakes that occur when the system doesn't behave exactly as the designers intended. Although digital chips give the impression that they're highly precise and rarely wrong, this is far from the truth. Errors happen more frequently than known and only error-correcting codes save us from knowing this.

Some codes will merely detect errors and then not even all of the time. Some modems and memory use 9 bits to store the normal 8 bits in a byte. The ninth bit is called the *parity* bit and it is set to be 1 if there is an odd number of 1's in the byte and 0 if there is an even number. If one bit is flipped by mistake, then the parity bit will not agree with the bits in the byte. But if two bits are flipped by mistake, then everything will seem correct.

Other codes are powerful enough to both detect errors and correct them. More parity bits can be added to create a system of equations that can be solved to reveal the real value. A common way to measure error-correcting codes is to say that they use m actual bits to represent n real bits of information and can detect p bits of error and correct q bits of mistake.

A popular metaphor for the error-correcting process is *sphere packing*. The codes for representing data are chosen by taking a collection of spheres and packing them into the space available. If you want to use m bits of error-correcting code to represent n real bits of information, then you need 2^n spheres that exist in an m dimensional space. Each sphere corresponds to one of the 2^n possible values for the n bits of real data. The error-correcting code version becomes the coordinates of the center of the sphere. So if sphere 23 is centered at point $(1, 0, 0, 1, 0, 1, 1, 0)$ then the error-correcting value of 23 is 10010110.

Why is the process called "sphere packing" instead of, say, "point arrangement"? The spheres indicate the margin of error. When the error-correcting code is converted back to the real value, then it doesn't need to match exactly. The closest sphere will do. Imagine that the value for 23 was mangled in transit and one bit was changed. 10010110 became 10110110. The distance between the point and the center is only one unit, so if sphere 23 has a larger radius, then it fits in and the error is effectively corrected.

Errors, however, are not randomly distributed. Some error-correcting codes can recover data from burst errors that mangle up to r bits in a row. These effectively spread out the data so that it is not concentrated in one position. These codes are common in radio networks that must recover from bursts of static.

Error-correcting codes are important tools for copyright protection because they can help defend against people who try to remove the tag. One popular approach for the attacker is to try and flip some of the least significant bits by either adding tagging information or simply adding new random data. Error-correcting codes can defend against this because they allow someone to recover the information even after some of the bits have been changed.

A Simple Example

Here's a simple example of a code that converts $n = 11$ bits of data into $m = 15$ bits of error-correcting code. If one ($q = 1$) of the $m = 15$ bits is changed, then it can be identified and corrected. The input bits are $a_1 \dots a_{11}$ and the output bits are $b_1 \dots b_{15}$. The code is much easier to understand, however, if binary subscripts are used: $b_{0001} \dots b_{1111}$.

The four extra bits are often called *parity bits* and they are constructed by using four simple equations. Here's a table. The extra bits are b_{0001}, b_{0010}, b_{0100}, and b_{1000}. Notice that each one has only a single "1" in its subscript.

The parity bits can identify which bit is wrong during the decoding process. Imagine that bit b_{1011} is flipped. This corresponds to a_{10} and

Output Bit	Where It Comes From
b_{0001}	$a_1 + a_2 + a_4 + a_5 + a_7 + a_9 + a_{11} \; mod \; 2$
b_{0010}	$a_1 + a_3 + a_4 + a_6 + a_7 + a_{10} + a_{11} \; mod \; 2$
b_{0011}	a_1
b_{0100}	$a_2 + a_3 + a_4 + a_8 + a_9 + a_{10} + a_{11} \; mod \; 2$
b_{0101}	a_2
b_{0110}	a_3
b_{0111}	a_4
b_{1000}	$a_5 + a_6 + a_7 + a_8 + a_9 + a_{10} + a_{11} \; mod \; 2$
b_{1001}	a_5
b_{1010}	a_6
b_{1011}	a_7
b_{1100}	a_8
b_{1101}	a_9
b_{1110}	a_{10}
b_{1111}	a_{11}

Table 5.1. This table shows the bits and the equations for building a simple error-correcting code.

a_{10} is part of the equations that determined b_{1000}, b_{0100}, and b_{0010}. These three values will not agree now that one error was introduced and the error can be located. This is the reason the subscripts were cast in binary.

This point is easier to see in the context of some equations that can be used to locate the error. These would actually be used by the decoding circuits to identify the location of any error.

$$c_0 = b_{0001} + b_{0011} + b_{0101} + b_{0111} + b_{1001} + b_{1011} + b_{1101} \ mod \ 2$$

$$c_1 = b_{0010} + b_{0011} + b_{0110} + b_{0111} + b_{1010} + b_{1011}$$
$$+ \ b_{1110} + b_{1111} \ mod \ 2$$

$$c_2 = b_{0100} + b_{0101} + b_{0110} + b_{0111} + b_{1100} + b_{1101}$$
$$+ \ b_{1110} + b_{1111} \ mod \ 2$$

$$c_3 = b_{1000} + b_{1000} + b_{1001} + b_{1010} + b_{1011} + b_{1100}$$
$$+ \ b_{1101} + b_{1110} + b_{1111} \ mod \ 2$$

The four values can be combined into the address of the bit that is bad. If b_{1110} is flipped, then c_3, c_2, and c_1 will be 1 and c_0 will be 0. If there is no error, then the values of c will be 0.

This scheme is straightforward and easy to understand because the parity bits were mixed into the right places. This system was set up to make the binary subscripts work in a simple manner. There is no practical reason why this level of simplicity needs to be carried through to general error-correcting systems. Many use more complicated schemes that correct multiple bits.

This system can correct $q = 1$ bits that are wrong. How many can it detect? Only $p = 1$. Imagine that two bits are flipped: b_{1010} and b_{1001}. The equation for c_3 will now return a zero instead of a one because the two changes cancel each other out. On the other hand, both c_1 and c_0 will both evaluate to 1, indicating that the error is in bit b_{0011}. Not only is this incorrect, but the answer is worse. Two bit errors in the values of b will produce three wrong errors in a: a_1, a_5, and a_6.

Periodic Error-Correcting Codes

Bursts of errors occur frequently in radio data and periodic codes are the most practical way to deal with them. They spread out the parity bits and the bits that they can correct. The last example placed the parity bits at positions b_{0001}, b_{0010}, b_{0100}, and b_{1000} to make the example easier to understand. Two consecutive errors could wipe out the entire system.

Periodic codes interleave several different systems of equations by shuffling them together. Two adjacent bits aren't part of the same sets of equations, so if both bits are flipped, then the answer can still be recovered. If there was no interleaving, then much of the mathematics is similar to the simple example shown before.

This periodic code inserts one parity bit for each block of s bits. It won't be able to correct the errors, but it will be able to detect bursts of up to $s - 1$ bits. Each blocks of bits, $S_{(i,1)} \ldots S_{(i,s)}$, is followed by parity bit B_i. More sophisticated versions could insert more parity bits to actually correct the error.

Here's an example of a bitstream with $s = 4$. The colons are inserted to indicate the beginnings and the ends of the blocks:

$$\ldots : 1 : 0001 : 1 : 0101 : 0 : 1110 : 0 : 0001 : 1 : 1111 : 0 : 1001 : 0 : \ldots$$

For the sake of simplicity, the first block shown in the bitstream, "0001", is $S_{(1,1)} \ldots S_{(1,4)}$. The parity bit after it, 1, is bit B_1. The first bit here is parity bit B_0.

What is the relationship between the parity bits and the blocks of data? Here's the equation:

$$B_i = S_{(i,1)} + S_{(i-1,2)} + S_{(i-2,3)} + S_{(i-3,4)} + B_{i-4} \bmod 2.$$

Every fourth bit is part of the same equation. The first three parity bits in the example above, B_1, B_2, and B_3, all rely on bits that were not displayed. The first parity bit that relies upon blocks that are shown is $B_4 = S_{(4,1)} + S_{(3,2)} + S_{(2,3)} + S_{(1,4)} + B_0 = 0 + 1 + 0 + 1 + 1 = 1$.

This code can survive bursts of up to three bits in a row and still report the correct answer because the bits in each equation are separated by three unrelated bits. Any burst of three consecutive errors will muck up three different parity equations and each will report an error. Here's the result of an error mucking up the first three bits in block S_4:

$$\ldots : 1 : 0001 : 1 : 0101 : 0 : 1110 : 0 : 1111 : 1 : 1111 : 0 : 1001 : 0 : \ldots$$

Now, the parity bits B_4, B_5, and B_6 don't agree. The errors leave a trail.

What if a parity bit is flipped by an error? The error will show up in two locations and point to two errors like a ghost. An error in B_5, for instance, will indicate an error in either $S_{(5,1)}$, $S_{(4,2)}$, $S_{(3,3)}$, $S_{(2,4)}$ or B_1. But it will also show up in the equation for B_9 and indicate an error there. This double set of errors indicates that a parity bit, not a regular bit, was flipped.

This code can detect bursts of up to 3-bit errors as long as there are five blocks of data (25 bits) between bursts. The code can't correct the errors, however, because it can't determine where the error actually occurred. Five bits feed into each parity bit and each of the five could have been responsible. If more parity bits are used, then a periodic code scheme can also correct errors.

Mirror Codes

Many standard error-correcting codes cannot recover if more than 50% of the bits are changed. This is a consequence of general information theory. These "mirror" codes can survive any arbitrary amount of changes in the bits, as long as the changes are evenly distributed and the number of changes is relatively consistent. This makes them an ideal tool for copyright protection because they can stand a large amount of deliberate tampering.

The basis for the codes are n dimensional cubes with 2^n corners. Figure 5.1 shows a three dimensional cube with the corners labeled with bits. The corner labels can also be thought of as the coordinates in three dimensional space. The number of bits of difference between two labels is known as the *Hamming distance* and it corresponds to the distance between two points if you travel along the edges of the cube.

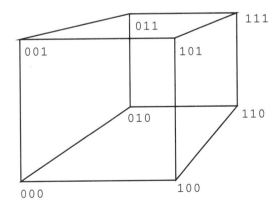

Figure 5.1. A three dimensional cube with the corners labeled.

Corners 010 and 110 are one unit apart while corners 010 and 101 are three units apart.

Cubes with an odd number of dimensions can be used as the basis for simple error-correcting codes. Begin with two opposite corners of the cube, which for simplicity will be 000 and 111. One of the corners will stand for "0" and the other for "1". If the cube has n dimensions and there are less than $\frac{n}{2}$ bits flipped, then the code can be interpreted correctly. The encoding of "0" as "000" and "1" as "111" can still be decoded if one of the bits is changed.

Although choosing the extreme corners with either all zeros or all ones may make the job of decoding simple, there is no reason why any two opposite corners can't be used. In fact, if the pairs are routinely changed according to some pseudo-random pattern, then it can add a degree of safety and security.

The cube-based codes can be used in many cases where a high degree of resistance to error is needed. They are not efficient because they take n bits to encode 1 bit, but they can resist up to $\frac{n}{2}$ changes. The problem occurs when more than $\frac{n}{2}$ bits are flipped. In these cases, the new code words are closer to the other corner and are better decoded as that corner.

Mirror codes resolve that problem with a second layer of coding. This layer replaces each "0" with either a "00" or a "11" and each "1" with either "01" or "10". This solution is the philosophical opposite of the cube. Instead of grouping the code words together according to which corner they are close to, the code words are kept far apart.

This solution has one important property: if both bits are changed in this layer, then the decoding is still correct. Changing "01" to "10" will still decode into a "1". This property is combined with the error-correcting property of cube codes to produce the mirror codes which can resist any amount of consistent bit flipping.

Here's a simple example using a five dimensional cube code. In the top layer, the bit to be encoded, "1", is converted into "10". In the bottom layer, each of these bits is replaced with 5-bit code words to produce: "1111100000".

These mirror codes will resist any arbitrary amount of bit flipping—as long as the bit flipping is uniformly applied in a consistent way. That means that if 90% of the bits are flipped in one part of the bit stream, then 90% of the bits must be flipped in all other parts of the stream.

This approach is far from perfect. If 50% of the bits are being flipped, then there is a good probability that more than $\frac{n}{2}$ bits will be flipped in one half and less than $\frac{n}{2}$ bits will be flipped in the other half. This can be resisted by increasing the size of n. When 90% are being flipped, then the odds are significantly lower that the mirror codes will decode incorrectly.

If the attacker is malicious, then the system can be strengthened by interleaving code words. This makes it less likely that an attacker will be able to flip bits in an inconsistent way.

Using Error-Correcting Codes

Copyright holders can use error-correcting codes in a number of different ways. The first is their intended purpose: to stop errors from occurring in their data. Most modems and network systems include error-correcting codes that will detect errors and ask for blocks to be resent. This is all transparently hidden from the programmer or the user. If you have particularly sensitive data, however, you might want to use a correcting code to catch even more errors.

If you use error-correcting codes, however, then you can also use the healing properties to tag data and identify different copies. Imagine that you flipped bit 1 in copy number 1, bit 2 in copy number 2, and so on. The error-correcting codes would catch this mistake and present the right data to the viewer, but if you wanted to identify the copy then you could check the data itself. The location of the error becomes the tag.

There are any number of arbitrary schemes for flipping these bits. You might want to use bits 1022, 10432, 12232, and 19010 as an arbitrary 4-bit counter. Errors in these locations can count between 0 (0000) and 15 (1111). In fact, error-correcting schemes can be layered on top of this. The 15 bit example from above could be used to embed 11 bits from a counter.

The errors do not always need to be in the same location. For instance, one set of 5 bits could indicate a 1 and another set could indicate a 0. The error could be in any of the first five locations and still indicate the same value: 1. The choice would be made at random. More and more of these sets could be aggregated to show a long value. Chapter 10 goes into much greater detail.

Error-correcting codes are also important building blocks for other tagging schemes. They can be added in as an additional layer to stop tampering. If someone tries to tamper with a number of tags, then the error-correcting codes can still reveal the correct answer if the tampering is minimal.

The hash functions described on page 30 are a form of error-detecting codes. Cryptographically secure versions are tamper resistant.

PRML-like Coding

Another common code used in data processing is called either *predictive response maximum likelihood (PRML)* or sometimes a *lattice* code. They are commonly used in hard disk drives to help disambiguate the data on the drive. They may be useful in many copyright tagging schemes where analog data may be available.

The best way to explain PRML codes is to explain the reason they make storing data on hard disk drives more reliable. The data is normally "written" on the magnetic medium by flipping an electromagnet on or off. The magnetic field leaves a magnetic footprint behind on the medium that can be detected later. The magnetic fields have two orientations, which are often called "north" and "south". In this context, it is much easier to think of them as fields with strengths $+5$ and -5. The value of 5 is chosen to avoid confusion with binary values because a 1 can be stored by creating a magnetic field with strength $+5$ and a 0 can be written by creating a field with strength -5. In reality, the value could be normalized by any constant.

A bitstream is stored on the magnetic medium by writing a sequence of magnetic dots with the right strength. The problem is that it is necessary to push the dots closer and closer together to pack more information onto a disk drive. Eventually, the dots begin to affect each other. If the two bits "1" and "0" are written close to each other in sequence, then the net result may be two dots with strengths $+3.2$ and -5. The writing of the second dot affected the first dot and drove it down.

PRML codes can decode this. For instance, imagine that the bitstreams 1000 and 0111 were written to disk. The first dot in each block of four bits would be affected by the three that follow it. In this example, the effects would be mirror images. The first dot in the first block might start at $+5$ and then be driven down to 0 by the writing of the subsequent dots of strength -5. In the second block, the opposite would happen. The first dot would start at -5 and be pulled up to 0.

Ordinarily a dot with value 0 would signal an error. The magnetic medium should read either $+5$ or -5. A zero might indicate that an impurity or some trauma had destroyed the ability of that location to read the value. A PRML code, on the other hand, would be able to determine just what happened by looking at the three bits that follow.

A Simple Example

Here's a PRML code. Each bit position, b_i, has two thresholds, h_i and l_i, indicating the high threshold and the low one. If the value at that position, v_i, is greater than h_i, then it decodes to a 1 and if it is lower than l_i, then it decodes to a 0. Anything in between is an error.

For simplicity, the value w_i is equal to $+5$ if b_i is 1 and -5 if b_i is 0. This corresponds to the value written by the drive head as it sweeps across the drive platter. Here's a sample equation:

$$h_i = w_i + .6w_{i+1} + .3w_{i+2} + .1w_{i+3}$$

Many PRML codes use particular polynomials with known factorization to improve the decoding process.

The decoding process involves trying to determine the best pattern of values for the w_i. There are several approaches, but the trellis algorithm is fairly optimal. It keeps track of the best possible interpretations of the data stream and then makes the final determination at the end.

The PRML codes are good examples of how to encode information that blurs together.

Tamper-Resistant Codes

Any tagging operation done with the coding process is vulnerable to attackers who may try to remove the tags or try to create a new file with tags that implicate some other user. Tamper-resistant codes help prevent this from occurring.

The simplest tamper-resistant codes include some part of a digital signature. A tag might include n bits of a serial number, S_i, corresponding to the rightful license holder for a document. This can be extended by computing some form of digital signature upon the n-bit tag and appending it.

The simplest digital signature can be formed with a digital hash function. The copyright holder appends a secret value, X, to the front of the serial number S_i, and computes $h(XS_i)$. Some of the bits from this result can be added to the serial number and added to the tags in the data. If an attacker recovers a document and attempts to create a new version with a fake serial number, S_j, the attacker won't be able to compute $h(XS_j)$ without knowing X. This prevents someone from implicating another person by coming up with a new tag.

The scheme can also use traditional public key cryptography to compute the signature. This has the additional benefit of easy verification. The copyright holder's public key can be distributed and users could verify the signature of S_i. This approach may be desirable if someone wanted to produce free copies of some very good compression software. The company might intend to make money by selling the compressing software to content producers while giving away the reader for nothing. If the reader looked for this tagged signature, then it could defend against others reverse engineering the compressing software. This result, however, requires substantially more bits because public key signatures often produce larger results.

Shaw's Codes

James Shaw presents an even more robust solution to prevent tampering in his Ph.D. thesis [Sha97]. He shows that it is possible to produce tagging codes that both prevent several users from framing another and also identify those users.

The codes rest on the assumption that two or more copies of a tagged document will find their way into an attacker. The attacker will be able to identify locations where tagging bits are stored by comparing the two or more files. The other locations where tagging bits are held, however, remain secret. His codes are set up so that the other tagging bits will positively identify both users.

The simplest implementation of his approach requires n bits for n users. The tag for user U_k is all zeros except for a 1 at the kth position.

The numbers 1 and 0 are used for illustration. In a real implementation, the actual value stored at the ith position would be XORed with some pseudo-random bitstream that would randomize the output. The best way to think about this is to imagine that the attacker can replicate the value found at position i or j or flip it to the opposite value, but the attacker can't know whether that bit at position i or j is a 0 or a 1.

Imagine that the copies for users U_i and U_j are recovered by the attacker. Comparison shows that the tagging bits are different at positions i and j. If the attacker tried to synthesize a new tag by leaving a 1 at both positions, then the new copy would implicate them both. They would not be able to implicate anyone else, however, because they would not know which other bits to flip. Shaw assumes that the tagging bits are randomly distributed throughout the data in order to reduce the chance that they'll be identified.

Of course, this approach has a 25% chance of going wrong. The pseudo-random scrambling would force the attacker to choose between writing 00 or 11 at the ith and jth positions. The scrambling means that he can't tell which is really which. If the attacker guessed to store 0's at both positions, he would produce a copy with no owners that couldn't be traced.

This can be avoided if k bits are used to mark the ownership for each person or kn bits to mark a set of documents for n people. Instead of simply placing a 1 at the ith bit position, k values of 1 could be placed at the k bits that make up the ith group of bits.

When the attacker grabs two copies of a document, then $2k$ bits will be different. The attacker must try to choose all $2k$ bits correctly. There is only 1 chance in 2^{2k} that the attacker will not leave one tagging bit in place and 1 chance in 2^k that the attacker will erase one owner's tag completely.

One interesting extension of this approach uses n^2 bits to mark documents for n users. n bits are marked at position i for user U_i by setting them all to 1. At the other $n - 1$ positions, all except the ith bit are set to be 0. The ith bit at position j is set to be 1 for all $j \neq i$. If an attacker comes across two copies, then there will be $2n - 2$ different bits. No amount of correct guessing will remove the mark.

These systems grow progressively weaker as the attacker gains better access to more and more copies. At two copies, the attacker can't be certain which document contained the 1 and which contained the 0 because of the pseudo-random scrambling. At three or more copies, the choices become obvious and it becomes obvious how to remove all of the marks.

Obviously, none of these methods are practical for large values of n. In his thesis, Shaw provides a more efficient approach based upon error-correcting codes.

Self-Synchronizing Codes

Many of the copy protection schemes depend upon accurately recovering both the tagging bits and the correct ordering. It is entirely possible that correct tagging bits will be recovered, but the ordering will be destroyed. Imagine, for instance, that an image is tagged with the license holder's ID number by repeatedly writing the ID number as the least significant bit of the pixels, one bit per pixel, starting at the upper left-hand corner of the image.

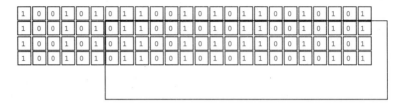

Figure 5.2. This Figure shows the least significant bits of an image file after writing the ID number 10010101 repeatedly. This sample is taken from the upper left-hand corner of the image so the number is easy to recover. The gray line is an imaginary cropping line that shows how the scheme could go awry.

If the entire document is found, then the ID number can be found again and again by starting at the upper left-hand corner and reading off the number bit by bit. Figure 5.2 shows a snippet from the upper left-hand corner. But if the image is cropped, then the position of the bits will be lost. It may be possible to recover the bits, but it may not be possible to figure out which is the first bit. Imagine that the image is cropped where the solid line is drawn. The wrong ID number, 01100101, would be recovered.

The simplest solution is to use self-synchronizing codes. One simple version designates one value of the 2^k values in a k-bit signal to be a start code, for instance, $000\ldots0$. The start of the bitstream is marked by writing the start code twice followed by a 1. If $k = 2$, then the start code is "00" and the start of the bit sequence can be found after the pattern "00001" is found. In this case, the ID number can be represented in less space if it is recoded in base $2^k - 1$ or base 3 when $k = 2$.

Summary

Coding techniques are some of the most important tools in a copyright defender's arsenal. Tagging documents in an imperceptible way is a great idea, but it is very fragile. If the tag introduces no perceptible change, then more imperceptible change could destroy it. Error-correcting codes are one defense. The algorithms from Chapter 10 for spreading out the data over a wide area of the data are another good defense.

This chapter has barely touched on many of the important areas of coding research. There are many books on the topics and the subject continues to be an area of active research. Serious users should feel compelled to dig deeper.

Chapter 6

Locking Data

This chapter explores several different ways that encryption can be used to lock up data and control who reads it.

The natural copyright defense is encryption, which is described, in introductory detail, in Chapter 2. Just lock up the data so it can't be read without the proper key. The data can be freely distributed through the cheapest channels and the short key can be supplied only when someone pays for the data.

The solution is relatively easy to apply and many companies use it to distribute their goods. Fonts, reports, and other data often arrive by CD-ROM, one of the cheapest ways to distribute data today. Each disk costs under $1.00, but it can contain plenty of expensive data.

This chapter is not really about designing encryption software to lock up the data—that's covered in Chapter 2. It is mainly about dealing with the other issues about packaging the data and minimizing the leaks outside the system. Both of these problems are more social than technical and a fair amount of customer sensitivity is required. The best system may not be the most secure one because it makes life so inconvenient for customers that they don't use it. Each business will need to make separate decisions about what is best for their customers.

Locking CD-ROMs

Locking CD-ROMs are quite common today. The Adobe collection of fonts is a great example and it is one of the most popular ways to

73

distribute the fonts. Graphics arts professionals can look at the different fonts available and purchase them by phone when they need them. The disk itself is not free, but Adobe includes some extra software (Adobe Type Manager) and several fonts with the purchase price. This saves them the cost of flooding the world with the disks like America Online at the price of potential sales.

The Adobe system is optimized to prevent people from giving unlocking codes to friends. Once the font is unlocked from the CD-ROM, it is stored on the hard disk ready to use. Someone could copy the font at this time or even mail it to friends, but there is little that can be done against this type of piracy. If people want to share data, they can do it.

The Adobe system merely minimizes the possibility of organized distribution by personalizing all of the unlocking codes. Each person needs a different unlocking code. This prevents people from collecting a list of unlocking codes for the disk and distributing it. These underground lists of unlocking codes are common in the video game world and there is no reason why they wouldn't proliferate in the font arena. This is the only major defense offered by the Adobe system.

This section examines how to build an Adobe-like system for locking data on the hard disk. It is not based on any actual knowledge of the guts of what Adobe does; it just explains how to achieve the same ends.

Customizing the Software

Customized locking codes can be generated by personalizing each version of the software. The software on the CD-ROM must be identical because it is pressed from a mold, but it can be personalized when it is installed on a hard disk. The installation program asks users for their name and a serial number, which usually comes on paper. The installation program converts this into a personalized number and either embeds it in the application itself or places it in a preferences file.

Cryptographically secure hash functions reduce data to short numbers in a tamperproof way. See page 30.

Some software packages also generate their own personalized ID by examining parts of the hard disk or the hardware. If a computer comes with an Ethernet card, then the Ethernet address is guaranteed to be a unique number. Other numbers are close to unique. The initialization date of the hard disk is often easy to access and there are few similar dates out there. This information can be customized by hashing it together with the user's name. The system may also just grab several blocks of data from the hard disk and hash them together. The hashing makes it fairly certain that each number will be unique.

There are problems with using machine-specific customization codes. Many people switch computers over time and they often want to take their old software to their new machine. Although some software is licensed on a CPU-by-CPU basis, most shrink-wrap software is sold by the copy. People feel free to carry it from machine to machine. A machine-specific ID could stop working when it is moved because the software won't find the right initialization date when it looks for the Ethernet address or other code.

The only way to avoid these problems is to generate the ID code once and store it with the software. If it is copied over to a new hard disk, then the ID code will go with it and all of the data will continue to work.

This customized code is often shipped directly to the main company at registration time. The new user may either read it over the phone, write it on a registration card, print out a registration form, or somehow send it over the Internet. If it is not sent in directly, then users must send it in each time they want to purchase some data.

Custom Unlocking Codes

Each file on the CD-ROM has only one true key that will unlock it. Call it K. The goal is to ship this to the local software in such a way that the user won't be able to write down K. Many CD-ROM access programs don't have automatic connections between the local software and the main company, so the unlocking code is often read out loud over the phone.

The easiest solution is to encrypt K with the ID and send $f_{ID}(K)$ as the unlocking code. Both the local software and the main company have access to ID, so they can exchange the value of K without reading it in the clear. If someone copies down the value of $f_{ID}(K)$ and gives it to a friend, it won't work because that friend has a different value of ID.

This system has a weakness that can be plugged. A clever individual could purchase all of the data on a CD-ROM and store the values read over the phone: $f_{ID}(K_1), f_{ID}(K_2), \ldots f_{ID}(K_n)$. If the encryption software is not secure, this may be enough samples to recover ID directly from these values. But most encryption algorithms are strong enough to resist this type of attack.

But the value of *ID* can be gathered in other ways. The user will often read it over the phone. Also, a skilled programmer will be able to use debugging software to trace the execution of the unlocking software. This will also reveal the value of *ID* and lead to the raw values of $K_1 \ldots K_n$.

The danger is that users will go into business for themselves. Now they know the values to unlock every file on the disk. They could generate new unlocking codes for their friends. When someone gives them their personal identification number, $ID(i)$, the keys could be rescrambled for them: $f_{ID(i)}(K_j)$.

The potential for this type of danger should vary from business to business. In many cases, it would be easier for users to make copies of the data outright for their friends than to go to the trouble of creating unlocking codes. But it may be conceivable that someone will go into business selling unlocking codes.

There is a defense. Each locking code can be encrypted with a different value, $X(i)$. This value could be generated in a number of different ways, but the simplest is to hash together *ID* and the date and time, $X_i = h(ID, time)$. The purchaser reads this value over the phone to the main company's representative, who types it into the computer. Then K_i is shipped over as $f_{X(i)}(K_i)$.

The approach can be made a bit stronger by having the user generate a random value, r_i, perhaps by hashing up the time code and some other data, $r_i = h(time, data)$. The user reads this value over the phone to the main company, which computes $X(i) = h(ID, r_i)$ on its own. Then the key is shipped as $f_{X(i)}(K_i)$. This forces the user to present a valid *ID*. The company can check its databases to make sure that the value of *ID* is registered correctly.

Public key algorithms can also be used. The key could be shipped using the recipient's public key. This is slower and not necessary, although it may become useful if a large public key infrastructure evolves.

Additional Details

The design of the software running on the user's computer can incorporate many different features. It may be desirable, for instance, to store all of the unlocking codes that were generated for a particular account. That would allow users to access the data on the CD-ROM using these codes in the future. They would not need to keep an extra, unencrypted copy of the data available on their hard disk. This can be a nice feature in many cases. Fonts, for instance, can take up plenty of room and they may be used sporadically.

The software can also be tuned to unlock each block of data only *n* times or only during a particular time window. This feature may be desirable from a marketing perspective and there is no reason why it can't be done. But it can also be circumvented fairly easily. People can keep an unencrypted copy of the data around and avoid unlocking it multiple times. The time feature can be easily avoided by changing the clock on the machine.

The main computer at the company may also want to keep track of the locking codes or the particular blocks of data that each customer purchased. If someone lost a copy of the data because of a hard disk crash or a theft, the company could issue a new copy of the unlocking codes for a minimal charge. This can build good will. I have taken advantage of this feature several times and I am always grateful for the chance.

Internet Locking

Data can also be delivered over the Internet in locked form. There are many companies that offer compression programs that also encrypt the data. Many people distribute their data by compressing it using these packages, placing the data on an FTP server or a Web site and then distributing the password as needed.

There is no reason why all of the algorithms described in the previous section on CD-ROMs can't be applied to delivering data over the Internet. Many of the conditions are similar. It is simple to place a large, public repository of data on an FTP server or a Web site in much the same way that it is possible to stamp out a large number of CD-ROMs. The data is not customized, but the same unlocking protocols used with CD-ROMs will deliver the same benefits.

The Internet, however, offers more advantages. If a computer is able to access a Web site, then it is often able to communicate directly with the publisher's main computer. This communication link can be used again and again, allowing the publisher to micromanage the user's access to the data. The data can be constantly locked up and users can be charged for every time they access the data. It could be allowed out only on specific days or during any arbitrary access scheme.

This link, however, can be problematic. Many people pay usage fees for access to the Internet. If they need to communicate directly with the data's publisher before each use, then they must connect to the Internet. This clogs up phone lines and restricts use. Also, the Internet may even be down. Links often fail. It is one thing to inconvenience the people who want to buy new data. It is another to shut down all users of your data.

Constant Monitoring

The user's software package can be customized in many ways. IBM is currently pushing a software concept called *Cryptalope*. They take the text data and encrypt it with a key. When people want to read the data, they supply their user ID number to the IBM central computer and it ships back the key. Each time they want to read the data, they pay again. A user must have an account with IBM, which handles the billing before paying a royalty to the data's owner.

This section does not describe the Cryptalope system in particular, but it does describe how to design a similar system with the same features. If you are a content creator and are looking for a running system, you may want to check out IBM's system.

The main difference between the CD-ROM systems and the Internet systems is the absence of a user in the loop. There is no particular reason why the publisher's computer can't ship the key, K, in the clear to the user's software. The user is not copying codes from the telephone into the computer, so the user can't easily give a copy of the key to a friend. A smart programmer will still be able to recover it, but it is still a challenge for most.

The publisher may still want to encrypt K for other reasons. Eavesdropping is not hard and there may be others on the Internet who want to recover the key. Automated programs may watch the traffic and grab all keys coming out of the publisher's machine. For these reasons, encrypting the keys with a customized user ID is a good idea. It costs little and adds more trouble for the data thief. Any wiretap of the publisher's computer will yield little usable data.

One important provision is making sure that not all of the information necessary to decrypt the file is exchanged over the network link. The best way to prevent this is to leave some customized identification data on the user's machine. This should be different from the ID and it should never travel over the Net. For instance, a user may have a number ID_i and a secret number B_i. This secret block may be established when a user opens an account.

When a user's program wants to get a key, it will identify itself with ID_i and include some unique transaction code, T. The key to the data, K, will be encrypted with another key, $X = h(B_i, T)$. Both the publisher's computer and the customer's computer know the value of B_i, but an eavesdropper doesn't know it. When $f_X(K)$ travels over the Net, the eavesdropper can't unravel it without B_i.

The unique transaction code is not necessary because the key could merely be encrypted using B_i. But it defends against more sophisticated attacks that can recover a key by analyzing multiple encrypted packets.

This approach uses hash functions because they are computationally cheap to use and unpatented. There is no reason why public key encryption systems can't be used instead. If a large, efficient certificate system evolves, then it may be quite reasonable to encrypt the key to the data with the user's public key.

Marketing Approaches

When the software is in place to unlock a chunk of data each time someone wants to access it, then there is a wide potential for strange and interesting marketing schemes. They are limited only by the inventiveness of the marketing staff, the patience of the users, and the time of the programmers who must develop the central computer dispensing the keys. Here is a list of some different schemes that might be used in the future.

Pay per Read The IBM Cryptalope system currently charges people each time they open up a document. If they turn off their machine at the end of the day, then they must pay again tomorrow.

This approach is quite simple, but it can be offensive. Many people are in the habit of reading printed material as much as they want. But if the price is reasonable, many people may not care too much.

Declining Costs per Access The central key server can keep track of how often a user accesses a document's key. Each trip could cost less. This would mitigate the problem of people turning off their machine before returning to the data as well as encourage buying in bulk.

Royalties If Bob gives Alice a copy of a document, then Bob may actually get a cut of what Alice pays to read it. This would encourage people to redistribute information and pass on data.

Implementing this would require adding a "read by" tag to each encrypted file of data. The user's software would need to read this data and pass it on to the publisher's computer so that it can properly pay the person who passed it on. This could create a long chain of people who pass on a document and it could generate royalties for all of them.[1]

One limitation to this scheme is the need to make the documents changeable. The data must be stored alongside the document for proper accounting. This prevents a person from merely passing along a URL or a pointer to a location in a database. Also, CD-ROMs are not writable, so the reader data can't be stored there.

Another solution is to simply embed a unique serial number in each copy of the document. There would be no need to have each document change to reflect who read it, but this information would need to be compiled at the main document billing site. It could then arrange to pay a user who reads copy x a royalty if someone else pays to read another copy of x. This system is really quite limited because it can't take advantage of a tree-like distribution pattern that might develop if each reader gave a copy to two people.

Crosslinking Deals An encyclopedia may contain a long summary describing a particular area and then offer links to more specific material. If a user reads the encyclopedia and then reads the special material, the encyclopedia's creator may get a cut of the royalty for referring them on.

These deals could increase the use of bibliographies and encourage authors to use them correctly. Many scientific bibliographies are often just lists of colleagues that are included more as a favor to the colleague than as a favor to the reader. If a reader discovers that most of the cross-references are worthless, then reader may stop following them. An author who accurately provides good extra material would be rewarded with more crosslinking royalties.

Weird Bulk Deals A writer may release a thriller at an increasing price scale. The initial chapters may be either free or quite cheap. The later chapters would increase in price and the one revealing the secret twist ending or the murder would be the most expensive. The central publisher's computer could keep track of the progress and charge accordingly.

---

[1] What an efficient chain letter! The money would be collected as people read the letter. There would be no need for them to send it in.

Each of these solutions can be implemented with a moderate amount of programming and a database. The simplest solutions don't require much of a user's history to be kept around. The more complicated, interrelated marketing schemes need access to a detailed history to determine the proper price. Although this historical record of a customer's choices may be cumbersome to implement and resonant with Big Brotherish worries, it is the simplest way to deliver complicated marketing. Many non-computer-based businesses regularly pay rewards for referrals and there is no reason why this won't become common as information proliferates in cyberspace.

Hardware Locking

The most sophisticated type of locking is done with standalone hardware known as either *dongles* or *smartcards*. Both devices are responsible for managing the keys necessary to access data. They are usually tamper-resistant and designed to prevent even the most sophisticated users from getting at the data without permission.

Turn to page 84 to see a discussion of how to break these schemes.

The dongles normally hang off one of the I/O ports of a microcomputer and jump in only when they detect a message coming their way. On the IBM PC, these are often found on the serial ports, and on the Macintosh they can be found sitting on the ADB (Apple Desktop Bus). In the future, as the PC adopts a Macintosh bus-like approach for these devices, dongles should be found on that bus as well.

Smartcards are credit-card-sized pieces of plastic with an embedded chip. They are used frequently in Europe to hold small balances for telephones and they're becoming common in the world of satellite television. The decoder for the satellite broadcasts won't work without the proper smartcard. Often, the smartcard contains the keys for a period of months and the company replaces it as needed.

Both the dongle and the smartcard contain a small computer chip with a small amount of flash memory that does not forget the information when there is no power. These chips can be programmed to accomplish much of what a desktop computer can do, but they are often severely limited by the amount of memory available. They are also generally rather slow and they don't have very wide data pathways useful for complex arithmetic.

The simplest and most successful use for smartcards is in the satellite television system. Here's a prototypical description of how it works. There is no reason why it can't be adapted to many other media.

Imagine that the smartcard will be used for three months, call them months 1, 2, and 3. The satellite broadcasters decide that there will be master keys for the months known as K_1, K_2, and K_3. In practice, the cards may also contain keys K_4, K_5, and K_6 to help in case the renewal cards don't arrive in time. These three keys are embedded inside the smartcard, which will have the job of decrypting messages encoded with the keys without revealing the keys to the user. If the keys left the smartcard, some clever guy might reprogram other smartcards and start selling them at a discount to undercut the satellite broadcaster.

This system is similar to Kerberos. See [MNSS87, SNS88, Koh90] and [BM91] for a discussion of its limits.

Each channel, show, or even segment could have its own key. For instance, *Cheers* would be broadcast under K_{Cheers} and the *Simpsons* could travel under the key $K_{Simpsons}$. The major problem is that each receiver doesn't know what the current key will be. The satellite system can't broadcast it directly because then pirates would also pick it up. The solution is to use the monthly key to hide it.

Just before *Cheers* begins, the satellite system would send a packet containing $f_{K_1}(K_{Cheers})$. Each receiver would hand this packet to the smartcard to decode it and return K_{Cheers}. Then the receiver could go about unscrambling the signal.

Key Management

The process of determining how and when to change the keys is largely a process of guesswork. If the keys are not changed that often, an underground market may develop that can grab the keys as they leave a legitimate smartcard and distribute them to illegitimate users. But if keys are changed too frequently, then it can be a synchronization headache.

Keys may also be distributed for separate packages. For instance, the satellite television systems may include special keys for decoding premium channels like HBO: $K_{1,HBO}$, $K_{2,HBO}$, and $K_{3,HBO}$. The extra keys can increase the marketing schemes available to the business, but there are practical limitations on the size of the memory available in the smartcards.

Each smartcard may also contain a customized key that is used only in one card. I.e. $K - Bob$ is found in Bob's smartcard. This allows the satellite system to turn on and off special channels. When Bob orders up a pay-per-view channel like one showing a fight, the satellite system sends out $f_{K-Bob}(K_{fight})$. Only Bob's card can decode this and recover the key.

This pay-per-view system could be used for all channels, but it is inefficient. One million users require one million keys to be broadcast. Bandwidth devoted to distributing keys can't be used to distribute programming.

Public Key v. Private

Most smartcard systems use private key encryption because it is significantly easier to compute. Most cheap smartcards can't do a good job with public key encryption at this time, but this will change. Public key encryption systems are also often patented and the licensing hassles can discourage people from using the technology if it isn't needed.

In this example of broadcasting information, there is little need for the features of public key encryption. There is not much need for either authentication or secure communication between parties that haven't met. The satellite feed is not in much danger of being stolen so there is little need for each decoding box to analyze the signal and determine whether it is authentic. If this was necessary, then a public key digital signature would be a good solution. While jamming and stealing control may be common in wartime and in comic books, it is unclear whether it is a serious threat for a commercial product like this.

Also, the satellites feed information in one direction only. There is no need for two decoders to set up a secure channel spontaneously. So there is no real use for a public key infrastructure.

There is no reason, however, why the approaches used in this section can't be adapted to public key encryption. If there is a widespread public key infrastructure, then it may be easy to use it to simplify matters.

Software Protection

Dongles are also used in software protection to stop people who ship around copies of a program. They may also use arbitrarily complex mathematics and encryption, but the typical solution is a challenge and response. Every so often, the program will create a challenge value, say x, and ask the dongle to return $f(x)$.

In practice, this is an ideal application for public key encryption using two functions: $E(x)$, for encoding, and $D(x)$, for decoding. The dongle contains $E(x)$ and the software has $D(x)$ written into it as a subroutine. The instructions in the software for computing $D(x)$ are generally easier for the attacker to read, but they are no help in determining the other half of the key used in $E(x)$.

Potential Leaks

Each of these systems provides some security to the owner of the data, but the security is always limited. If the data is going to be sold to someone and displayed on the screen, then there is the potential that someone will make a copy of that data. There is a number of possible attacks that range between simple and exceedingly clever and some are impossible to defend against. Although there is no perfect defense, many of the attacks require more time and effort than the cost of the underlying data. This makes it entirely likely that the attacks will be few and not add significantly to the bottom line.

The simplest attack is the screen shot. If the data is on the screen, then a photograph can be taken of it. There is no way to stop this attack and there may never be a successful solution. In fact, many bootleg videos of movies exist because people take a video camera into the theater and tape it.

Also, many operating systems have a feature for taking a screen dump and this feature is embedded at a low level. Disabling it is usually not possible. Some operating systems also allow other screens to receive copies of a master screen. This software is often used to help people debug their systems and it is also a major part of groupware. These software level tools will probably become more and more common as time goes by.

Each of these features makes it easy for many people to read what is on the screen. Some computers will never have these features and it may become quite easy to restrict their use on some machines. Some computers may offer only a limited set of features like displaying Web documents. These machines would probably not need the ability to make screen dumps and the manufacturers may even choose to disable the feature in order to strengthen the hand of content providers. Strong copyright protection could help them sell machines by encouraging more data to be available.

Low-Level Access

If an attacker can enter the lower realms of the system software, then another wide range of attacks can become possible. The collection of subroutines used to draw information on the screen can be changed or patched to leak copies of the data. A routine for drawing the characters on the screen is called to display all of the letters in the text. If this routine also saved a copy of the letters to disk in the process of drawing to the screen, then a copy would now be available.

This type of low-level hacking can defeat many encryption schemes. If the data arrives in encrypted form, the smartcard and the encryption software will decode the data for display. An eavesdropper who listened in on the network link would get only encrypted data, but a low-level patch on the drawing code would get the information in the clear.

There are several defenses against this approach and they will only slow down the attacker. The first is to scramble the display of the letters on the screen. That is, draw an "e" in the upper left-hand corner, a "q" in the lower middle, and continue in a haphazard fashion until the screen is filled. This may look strange, but it would force the attacker to keep track of the coordinates to unscramble the text.

The second solution is to embed custom drawing routines inside the software. Some high-end producers may want to do this anyway to produce cool displays. Anti-aliased text is easier on the eye, but many OSs don't offer it. Custom fonts are also nice and they may not be installed on each system. Bundling them with the data can remove licensing problems and ensure that each user will have them available.

Custom drawing routines, however, will probably be accessible to the attacker. A clever programmer should be able to spot these routines and attach another patch. This is not as easy as patching the built-in routines of the OS, which (usually) come with documentation. In fact, a weird collection of multiple routines could make this difficult to attack.

Of course, the ultimate attack against any text display on the screen is to grab a copy of the screen and use algorithms from optical character recognition software on the bitmaps. The characters should be identical and easy to disambiguate. Good OCR software can easily hit 99.5% on scanned-in data. There is no reason why it can't approach 100% on screen dumps.

Attacking Programs

Software protected by dongles is also relatively easy to defeat. The software must communicate with the dongle by writing data out of a standard I/O port. This code is simple to spot. A clever programmer will identify this part of the program and determine where the dongle's return information is kept. The simplest attack is to look for the part of the program that checks to see if the dongle spoke correctly. The final test can be inverted so that it accepts only incorrect answers from the dongle.

There is little that can be done against this level of attack. In many cases, software companies try to forbid it with their usage license. They force the user to agree not to disassemble or reverse engineer the software. This is certainly not practical to enforce, although it might be useful if some witness decided to snitch.

Grabbing Keys

Another important attack is grabbing the encryption keys. A smart programmer can also patch parts of the OS or the program to allow them to pause the program and grab the encryption keys from memory. If the data is available to the computer, then it is usually accessible to a clever programmer. The keys must be available to the computer.

The value of this attack may be limited. Consider the CD-ROM system used to distribute fonts. It would not be too hard to scan the Adobe software and determine where the keys for decoding the fonts are kept. A copy can be stored to the hard disk and distributed quickly.

The keys, however, may be of little use to the average user. The software requires a different, customized key for each font. Average users need to type in the customized values for their computers. Although it would be possible to distribute software that did this, it would be hard to distribute a list of the keys.

The value of the keys is also limited by the value of the data. Once the font or the data is unlocked, a copy is often available on the hard disk. Most basic users can make a copy of this font and distribute it. The key locking system just prevents them from easily accessing all of the data on the disk.

In some situations, the keys are much more valuable and that is why smartcards are used. The monthly keys for satellite channels, for instance, would be much more valuable if they were distributed. The smartcards are tamper-resistant so the keys would not be available in the general part of the memory.

Attacks on Smartcards

Smartcards can be attacked in a number of different ways. Physical approaches are common. The layers can be stripped away and the data may be recovered. It is not clear what the state of the art is in this arena, but it seems unlikely to me that either the attacker or the smartcard manufacturer will ever have the upper hand. The future will probably be a game of cat and mouse where the manufacturers develop one level of defense and it remains secure until someone uncovers a way around it. The widespread availability of machines that will detect atoms and their electric fields makes it unlikely that the manufacturers will be able to mount any real defense.

This book cannot offer any deep discussion about the physical security of smartcards.

More recently, mathematical attacks against smartcards were widely discussed. Dan Boneh, Richard DeMillo, and Richard Lipton of Bellcore showed how to recover an RSA key from inside the smartcard if the smartcard could be forced to make mistakes. Errors can be induced by bombarding the card with radiation, although it is unclear how much is necessary and if it can be controlled.

The attack was extended to DES by Eli Biham and Adi Shamir using a variant of their differential cryptanalysis. Ross Anderson and Markus Kuhn also showed a different approach that yielded the same result.

These results can be defended against by having the smartcard test its answers before releasing them. This can prevent enough useful data from leaking to the attackers. There is considerable evidence that the smartcard designers knew of these types of attacks long before the current spate of public discussion. Some hardware implementations for DES, for instance, were specifically designed to test the data before releasing it.

There can be interesting leaks in the strangest places. Paul Kocher showed how to extract an RSA key by timing the encryption. This can be defended against by adding random padding and delays.

There can never be absolute proof that a smartcard or any computer system for that matter will ever provide complete security. The greatest problem may be that any of the major encryption systems could prove to be insecure. A clever insight could make it simple to factor large numbers and cripple RSA. Brute force machines are becoming more common. Vigilance is the only option against the process of time.

Summary

Encryption is a powerful tool for locking up data. It protects the information while it is moving throughout the network and it also protects it from some of the simplest attacks. Many computer users can read basic files and copy them, but they don't know what to do to read encrypted files. This hurdle is enough to keep most users honest. As long as the cost of the data is less than the cost of breaking the encryption system, then people will behave correctly.

Additional solutions from other parts of the book may also be relevant. The unlocking software can also customize the data as it places it on the disk. The CD-ROM font unlocking software, for instance, could embed the ID number of the user in the font. A clever attacker would need to spot this and remove it. If a copy of the font was found, it could be traced back to the person who originally bought the font. Illegitimate copying could be punished through the court system.

Most of this book suggests ways to add tags to pictures, text, and other data. Many can be quite hard to detect and prevent. These make an ideal complement for unlocking systems because the tags can be added before the data is placed on the screen. Any screen-scraping program or low-level patch would copy the individualized tag.

Chapter 7

White Space

Printed text documents are easy to manipulate and information can be hidden inside the white space. This chapter explores some of the schemes for sending a 1-bit message by fiddling with the layout.

The Space Cadet

Gotham City was troubled by strange occurrences on the Internet for two weeks before the Space Cadet released his manifesto. At one point, a large scaffolding set up around a downtown building began to fail and the police dispatched an urgent e-mail message, "Send Carpenter Now." They were flabbergasted when a large truck from the fish market rolled up. Everyone thought it was a simple glitch that had converted the message to "send carp enter now." The manifesto, however, explained that it was the work of the Space Cadet's virus, which he had released to the world to satisfy his political ends. Here is the beginning of the manifesto:

They say it is emptiness, nada or filler. It's valueless. It's marginalized. It's ignored time and time again. This humble breather, this subtle pause of relaxation, this moment for reflection and introspection, this small interruption in blather, this silent injection of peace, this meditation on the importance of nothingness, this grace note, this lowly space.

Children in grade school don't even learn that it is the most important part of the alphabet. There is no special cursive version of it. The space between words, however, is not nothing—it is something. Something important and vital that defines by what it is not. It is not a word and by this very reason it gives the words their beginning and their end, the marking of their meaning.

For all of these reasons and many that go unsaid, as is the case in every message conveyed by the emptiness between words, the space must be liberated. It must be raised to be the equal of the words themselves. This will restore the cosmic balance to the world...

Hiding White Space

Text documents have plenty of white space between words and lines and the amount of this white space can be subtly modified to hide the tagging information that could identify the owner. The spacing between words that is used to justify text can be modified in a unique way. The location of the lines on the page can also be changed in small ways that encode a message. All of this white space is fair game.

The main advantage of using the empty sections to encode data is that the text does not need to be changed. Chapter 8 describes how to modify the text documents themselves by changing the words. This is not easy to do well and in many cases it is impossible to change even one letter in the document without changing the integrity of the document. The white space, however, can be modified without changing the meaning of the document.

The disadvantage of this approach, however, is that it is easy to remove the tagging information by reformatting the document. A paper document can be scanned and converted into an electronic text file through optical character recognition. A text file with hidden characters could be inadvertently cleaned up by any careful program. Many software programs will simply strip away the old formatting on the way to creating their own and this will remove the tagging information.

The rest of this chapter will describe approaches for modifying the white space in a text document to encode information. Some of the approaches are good for both paper printouts and ASCII text files that float around a network like the Internet. Others are useful only for printouts.

Hidden Characters

There are 256 possible ASCII text values and 65,536 UNICODE values, but there are only 26 letters in the English alphabet. Even with punctuation and characters modified by accents, there may be only about 90 or fewer printing characters. The other values are often ignored and unprinted. These characters can be inserted in locations to store bits.

For instance, it is possible to think of each of the breaks between words as a location like a pixel. One bit can be hidden at this location by the presence or absence of a non-printing character. Two bits can be hidden if there are three non-printing characters available to be inserted. More bits are certainly possible. The bits hidden at these locations can be grouped together to store larger blocks of data using all of the techniques described in Chapter 10. All of the techniques for encoding longer files in the least significant bits of a pixel file can also be used here.

The greatest threat to this technique is the lack of consistency between various software programs. Each one will often handle non-printing characters differently. Some word processors will simply skip over them. Others will replace them with a standard space. Still others will have a special character, like a square, that takes their place on the screen. You may compose your markings in software that doesn't display a particular character and someone else may read it with software that does.

For all of these reasons, this solution is really recommended only for very limited environments where the behavior of the software is well understood. It may be possible to use this approach inside Lotus Notes where all of the people run the same software suite, but it would be dangerous to even contemplate the possibility that all of the Internet will treat hidden characters in the same way.

Hidden characters are also used on Web pages to fool the webcrawling indexing programs like Alta Vista. Authors often include key words like "sex" and have them displayed in the same color as the background so the reader won't see them. The search engine, however, will register the word and direct all searches for it to that Web page. This approach is becoming problematic and webcrawlers are trying to thwart it.

Extra Spaces

Extra spaces can be added in unobtrusive locations. The end of each line can support several extra spaces without leaving any indication to the reader that there is anything there. A simple encoding scheme discussed in [BGML96] simply adds extra spaces at the end of each line. The number of spaces must be done in some simple coding scheme. For instance, adding no spaces might qualify as a "0" and one space would qualify as a "1". More spaces could also be used, but the effectiveness drops.

Naturally, any scheme like this can easily be destroyed by reformatting, which may be done automatically by many programs on the network looking to save bandwidth. Printing the information is also an easy way to lose these white space characters. This scheme would work only with text in electronic form.

Justification

Most of the professional text is justified so that both sides of a column of text are flat and look clean. This effect is produced by inserting extra amounts of white space throughout the line until the last character is flush against the right margin. There are a number of different schemes for doing the justification and each of them can be modified in a few simple ways to encode some information.

The basic algorithms will add the same amount of white space at each space along the line. For instance, if there were five spaces in a line and the line was coming up 12 mm short, then 2.4 mm of space would be added between each pair of words. The most sophisticated justification algorithms will add more white space after the sentences. TeX does this and so do many of the other good programs. This extra space after the sentence is often considered both aesthetically pleasing and a bit of extra emphasis for the end of a cogent thought.

The simplest solution is to change the distribution of white space. Instead of spreading it out equally, it can be doled out to the interword gaps in slightly different amounts to leave a trail of information. The success of this approach depends upon the precision of the text rendering device (usually the printer) and the precision of any detection device (usually a flatbed scanner).

Printers and scanners often come with promises from the manufacturer that they deliver 600 dots per inch resolution. These claims must be viewed with some suspicion by anyone trying to hide information, because they don't mean that it is practically possible to move letters a 600th of an inch and then detect the move. The greatest problem is that flatbed scanners often generate their high resolution by interpolating. This may make it difficult to detect letters that have moved. Printers may often fail to have such precision because toner can bleed and fill in gaps.

The eye can also detect remarkably small changes in spacing, especially if they are part of a regular pattern. Small changes in the amount of white space between words are harder to notice than small changes in the distances between lines. The gaps between words are already affected by the shapes of the letters and they are far from exact. For instance, the gaps between "my way" and "spam king" are different because one gap is defined by letters with a slanted edge and the other is defined by letters with a vertical stroke. The interline gaps, on the other hand, are more consistent because English text presents a fairly strong lower edge.

The simplest scheme is to modify each word space in a line. Define the minimum amount of white space that can be added and subtracted from an interword space and be successfully printed and recognized later. Let this be s mm of space. Here are the steps:

1. Justify the line. Assume there are n gaps between words.

2. Encode $n-1$ bits into the first $n-1$ gaps by adding $\frac{s}{2}$ mm of white space to the gaps that will encode a 1 and subtracting $\frac{s}{2}$ mm of white space from the gaps that will encode a 0.

3. Use the last gap to rejustify the line by adding up the 1's and the 0's and adding or subtracting the right amount, ($\frac{s(ones-zeros)}{2}$).

4. Alternate between using the first and the last gap to rejustify the line. That is, on one line put all of the extra white space padding at the left and on another put all of the white space padding at the right.

If the tagging bits being encoded are well distributed and have equal numbers of ones and zeros, then this algorithm will perform fairly well. The expanded gaps will often cancel out the shrunken gaps and the last gap will not have much need to add or subtract padding. Nevertheless, a run of ones will force all of the gaps at the beginning of the line to be expanded and this will remove a substantial amount from the last gap. It could easily be too much to be represented and bring the two words together.

The best solution is to limit the number of bits that can be encoded in each line.he ideal number depends upon the size of the line and the distribution of the tagging data.uwie If there are significant runs of zeros or ones, then the limit should be set short. Fully random data, however, can pack more into a line.

Another solution to significantly long runs of zeros or ones in the tagging data is to XOR the tagging data with the output of a random

The exclusive-or (XOR) operation is simple: 0 XOR 0 = 0, 0 XOR 1 = 1, 1 XOR 0 = 1, and 1 XOR 1 = 0.

number generator. This will remove any long runs and also help hide the tagging data. If the random number generator is cryptographically secure, then it can also add encryption. Of course, encrypting the tagging data with an algorithm like DES will also remove long runs of zeros or ones in almost all cases.

Justifying through Ratios

Changing the size of the spaces throughout a line may not be possible to do well in some cases. The scanners may have a limited resolution, making the amount of change rather large. If it is large enough, the eye can easily pick it up and it may make the text look ugly.

Another solution can encode only one bit per line, but it is much more manageable. Many text formatting programs will stretch the space after a punctuation mark more than the space between ordinary words. TEX, the system used to create this book, will stretch the space after a comma by 1.25 the amount of spacing between words. Space after a period, a question mark, or an exclamation point will stretch 3 times more than the interword space. Here's an example:

"Go! Fight! Win!" screamed Marci, a cheerleader.

"Go! Fight! Win!" screamed Marci, a cheerleader.

"Go! Fight! Win!" screamed Marci, a cheerleader.

"Go! Fight! Win!" screamed Marci, a cheerleader.

There is no reason why the space after a punctuation mark couldn't spread at merely double the rate of the interword spacing. The spreading formula could be changed from line to line to send information. This modulation would be quite effective and may not be too visible to the eye. TEX already does strange things when it can't fill out a box.

This level of steganography demands access to the source code of the typesetting program. TEX is widely available and ready to be modified.

Justifying ASCII Text

Pure ASCII text is still common on the Internet. Most of the USENET newsgroups carry simple ASCII with little extra formatting commands. In these situations, the authors will often format the ASCII by adding either spaces or blank lines. The effect of this is normally fine for the casual nature of the USENET, but the crudeness makes adding tagging information more of a challenge. It just isn't possible to move a word or a section of text over by a barely perceptible smidgen. The minimum size is a space.

The justification algorithms for ASCII text depend upon a *monospaced font* that dispenses the same amount of space to each letter whether it is an "i" or an "m". The algorithms count how many characters are in a line and then determine how short the line may be. The extra space from the end of the line is parceled out as spaces between the words.

Information can be encoded in the places where the extra spaces are added. If there are m gaps between words and n extra spaces to be parceled out, then there are $\binom{m}{n} = \frac{m!}{n! \cdot (m-n)!}$ different ways that the spaces can be added. For instance, if there are 5 gaps and 3 extra spaces to be added, then there are $\binom{5}{3} = \frac{5 \cdot 4 \cdot 3}{3 \cdot 2 \cdot 1} = 10$ different ways that they can be inserted.

The greatest challenge is finding a simple way to convert the tagging data into the location of the spaces and to recover it later. If there are 10 different ways that three spaces can be added to five gaps, then one complete digit could be stored in the process of adding the spaces. In base two, three bits is the maximum that could be stored here, but it will choose between only eight different values. One simple solution is to round off the data and simply ignore the other two choices in this case.

Another solution is to use a flexible radix system. Most standard radix systems use the same base for each of the "digits" or "bits". That is, in base 10, the value of each digit is a power of 10. The least significant digit is worth 10^0, the next digit is worth 10^1, etc. In base two, the bits are worth powers of two.

A flexible radix system, on the other hand, is worth a different amount at each position. Let a_i be the radix of position i with $i = 1$ being the least significant position. In normal base 10 notation, $a_i = 10$ for all i. The value of each position, A_i, is

$$A_i = \prod_{j=0}^{i-1} a_j$$

To be complete, $a_0 = 1$.

The value at each position i, b_i, can range between 0 and $a_i - 1$. The value of the number is:

$$\sum_{i=1}^{n} b_i A_{i-1}$$

The value of the entire number can be calculated from this formula. A number in standard radix can be converted into this flexible radix with the standard process. The value of b_i is calculated by dividing the number by A_i and repeating the process recursively on the remainder.
Here's a short example:

Line	Gaps to Be Filled	Extra Spaces to Be Added	Choices (a_i)
l_0	5	3	10
l_1	6	2	15
l_2	4	3	4
l_3	5	5	0
l_4	7	5	21
l_5	5	2	10

Line l_3 can't contribute anything to the process of hiding information, so it is ignored. The values of A_i can be computed from the a_i. Let the tagging value be 101,743 in base 10. If it is converted into this flexible radix system, the values of b_i are:

i	A_i	b_i
0	1	3
1	10	4
2	150	2
3	600	0
4	600	1
5	12,600	8

The values of b_i must be encoded in lines l_i. That means the first line (l_0) must accept three extra spaces in five gaps in a way that represents the number 3. The second line must convey the value "4", the third line, "2", the fourth line does nothing, etc.
The process for embedding a value in a line is not simple. There are no easy formulas known to the author. The simplest suggestion is to enumerate the possible combinations in a set order and choose the combination in that order. For instance, the three spaces can be placed

in five gaps in the following combinations: 123, 124, 125, 134, 135, 145, 234, 235, 245, 345. To encode the number "3" in line l_0, place spaces in the first, third, and fourth gaps. The number "9" would places spaces in the third, fourth, and fifth gaps.

This process of actually listing the gaps is not efficient for large collections, but it may be manageable for smaller numbers like those found in the process of hiding information in text. If there are only seven or eight gaps in a line, then the computation is manageable.[1]

A Simpler Scheme

Walter Bender, Daniel Gruhl, Norishige Morimoto, and Anthony Lu present a simpler approach for ASCII text in [BGML96]. Their scheme adds bits in pairs of successive spaces and each bit requires two inter-word gaps. This limits the scheme when there are short lines or many spaces to be added to justify the right-hand side. For instance, in most cases with longer lines, there may be four extra spaces and 10 inter-word gaps. In their scheme, the first eight interword gaps would be used to add the four extra spaces and four total bits would be encoded in the process.

The algorithm is simple. If the first gap in a pair gets the extra space, then a "1" is encoded. If the second gap in the pair gets the space, then a "0" is encoded. This spreads the extra spaces along the line, to some extent, but it often does not use the full length of the line.

If there are n interword gaps and more than $\frac{n}{2}$ spaces to be added, then their approach cannot be used successfully.

PostScript

Adobe's PostScript language is one of the most used systems for carrying the printing instructions to a printer. The language is a stack-based language using plain ASCII text. The various commands will handle the basic drawing primitives like drawing a line, plotting a curve, or drawing a character from an alphabet in a particular font. The commands are rendered at the best resolution of the printing engine.

The designers of the language anticipated that PostScript users would focus a great deal of their energy on positioning letters upon

---

[1] If anyone knows of such a formula for finding the ith selection without calculating all $i-1$ selections, let the author know. It must involve some recursion.

the screen, so they included several different operators to make this job easier. The basic function, show, will draw some letters at the current position of the pen. Consider this code:

```
240 moveto
(Hello World!) show
```

This code will move to coordinates (100,240) and draw the string "Hello World!" The coordinates are normally measured in terms of points (1/72 of a inch) from the lower left corner of the page. The commands come after the parameters because the language is stack based. This will not have any effect on the short examples shown here, but it makes many parts of the process of writing code for the screen substantially easier.

Another modified version of PostScript will do some simple kerning. The command widthshow will add a particular amount of space after one particular character, which is usually the space. This can be used easily to justify a line by adding the extra amount between words. Here's some code:

```
240 moveto
(Normal Interword Spacing) show
210 moveto
0 8#040 (More Interword Spacing) widthshow
```

The second line will get an additional nine units added to the horizontal width of the character with the code "8#040", which happens to be the space in base 8. There is no extra width added to the vertical spacing. This means that the second line will have 18 units added to the two spaces, making the line 18 units longer than if it had been set with the plain show command.

A third PostScript command, kshow, may be the most usable. It will execute an arbitrary procedure after each character is drawn. This would allow you to create arbitrarily complex kerning schemes for laying out the page. After each character is drawn in the string, it will push onto the stack both the character and the next character to be drawn. The procedure can pop these values and move the position of the pen accordingly.

The process of writing PostScript routines is beyond the scope of this book. It is not conceptually difficult to imagine writing a routine that would store a vector of values in an array and then walk through this vector and use the data to permute the amount of space allocated to each interword gap.

Experimental Bounds

Jack Brassil, Larry O'Gorman, Steve Low, and Nicholas Maxemchuk provide excellent insight into the practical limits on the amount of information that can be shipped by moving letters and words a small amount [BO96, BLMO95, LMBO95]. They frame the problem of hiding information as "expanding the bounding box". Many digital typesetters place a bounding box around each letter and then lay these bounding boxes on the page as a bricklayer puts down bricks. They suggest that an easy way to layer steganography on top of typesetting programs is to expand the bounding box an imperceptible amount and then wiggle the letter around the box to encode information. If the letter is shifted to the left, it means a "0", for instance.

Their experiments show that the bounding box can be expanded as little as 1/300 of an inch and the difference will still be noticeable by a scanner even after photocopying and other minor degradation. They produced their documents on a printer with the resolution of 600 dots per inch and used a scanner that was accurate to 1/1200 of an inch. Some words on line would be shifted up or down by two pixels and this would encode the information.

They report that the most important job is aligning the paper on the scanner in order to reduce the amount of deskewing that is required. If there is a heavy amount of deskewing required, then a fair amount of distortion will be added to the image by the rotation algorithms. Even when the alignment is strong, there still may be a pixel or two of error introduced in the process of trying to align the baseline up with the pixel grid. The process of rotating a bitmap is complicated.

The algorithms in Chapter 10 can be used to encode files in these shifts.

They also report that the success of the system can be increased by choosing the shifted words and fonts carefully. Fonts with serifs provide stronger lines along the baseline of a word than sans-serif fonts. Words with strong serifs along the bottom like "mailman" are easier to spot than words with softer bottoms like "you". Letters like "y" or "g" also break up the baseline in a word.

Shifting the words left to right is much easier to do. The eyes seem to be even less sensitive to variations in the amount of space in between the words.

The results of their experiments are quite encouraging. They report that they found one of the best solutions was to move words up and down in the middle line of a group of three. This provided enough information to find the baseline in as accurate a way as possible.

Summary

The vast areas of white space on each page are candidates for encoding information on the printed page. Today's laser printers have more than enough resolution to do a great job moving words a fraction of an inch and today's scanners can detect this movement successfully. Practically every part of the page is fair game for a nudge here and a push there.

The greatest impediment is the lack of standard typesetting methods for doing this. None of the standard packages offer this as an option. PostScript offers enough resolution, but many word processors or typesetting programs spit out completely different PostScript. It is not really practical to write one program that reinterprets the PostScript from all sources and adds the tagging information

Nevertheless, it is possible to do this coding by hand. Perhaps time will yield software to do it automatically.

Chapter 8

Mimic Functions

One of the most sophisticated ways to embed information in a document is to change the words. This chapter explores some of the grammar-based mimic functions and their security.

Gallery Talk

The scene is a Manhattan art gallery.

Owner: Good afternoon. May I say, "Welcome"?

Customer: Sure. You have some wonderful pieces here.

O: You must be mistaken. Our wonderful pieces are over in the other wing. This section is strictly devoted to the beautiful and the exquisite.

C: Oh. Why aren't these wonderful?

O: Well, to the uneducated eye they might seem "wonderful", but the artist has gone beyond that phase in his exploration of the painting medium. Today, he's strictly interested in evoking the beautiful and teasing it into existence on his canvas.

C: So what makes this one "beautiful"?

O: The artist wants to summon the spirits of pure, elegant form and a shameless devotion to reformed hedonism and arrange for them to swirl upon the canvas in a rapturous ballet. He's interested in synthesizing an uneasy peace between the forces of decadence which rule the left bank, if you will, of this canvas and the armies of innocent pleasure that dominate the right side of the picture. The harmony of this ersatz chorus consists of a harp section plucking notes in the key of spring-time while the horns echo the melodic line with a cynical devotion to pleasure that can only come from a long-term life on Earth.

C: Oh.

O: Yes, I suppose it is understandable that you've confused them with the "wonderful" pieces. It's a simple distinction, but one that takes a certain devotion to the form.

C: Oh.

O: Yes, the wonderful works we have in the other wing trade upon their ability to evoke the sense of impossible glory. In a sense, the artist wanted to capture the emotion that grazed across the synapses of Dorothy and her retinue when she first came into the chamber of the great Wizard of Oz. In another, he wanted the viewer of the painting to understand the elation that washed over the fans when the U.S. Olympic hockey team won the gold medal in 1982.

C: This canvas is certainly exquisite.

O: You don't listen, do you? This is a beautiful work.

C: I thought you said that they were "beautiful and exquisite" in this room.

O: Some are one, some are the other and some are both. This one is merely beautiful. There is none of the exotic taste of cinnabar and coriander that permeates his exquisite works. This is strictly sweet cream and mint.

C: Well, okay. How much does it cost? I'm sure it's not insignificant.

O: In a sense it is "insignificant" when you compare it to the sadness it can replace in your heart. It's more an "elegant" price that is over-shadowed with a soupçon of chthonic fear that whispers the threat of debtor's prison . . . .

Changing Words

Personalizing a text document can take place on two different levels: the hidden and the overt. The process of including "invisible" tags or information is described in Chapter 7 and it can provide a good solu-tion if the attacker doesn't look for the tags. Text files are often fairly simple and succinct, so there are few places to add hidden information without it standing out to an educated eye. For instance, much of the text posted on the Internet is raw ASCII. Extra spaces, tabs, or white space characters serve no purpose and anyone who found them could easily strip them out.

Another solution is to hide the personalization information in the open. Ironically, it is much harder for an attacker to identify the tagging information in a document if it is incorporated into the document itself. The tags could be constructed by choosing adjectives from a particular collection. In one version of the document, a dancer would be described as "sleek" and in another "graceful." If these changes are made systematically, then a wide array of documents can be tagged in large quantities.

There are obvious limitations to changing the actual text of the document. Many environments like the law have such a large emotional attachment to exact replicas that they could not tolerate even minor changes. The process also demands some precision and probably can't be completely automated. Alternating between "sleek" and "graceful" may be acceptable in some situations, but words like "fly" have multiple meanings and computers may not get the nuances correct.

This chapter will explore modifying the text with a variety of schemes. Some are simple and others are more complicated and extravagant. Many people may be satisfied with the simpler solutions, but the more elaborate ones are included in case people need a more robust solution.

Swapping Words

The simplest way to hide information in a text document is to change some of the words. Flipping between two different words will effectively add one bit of tagging information to the document in the same way that the techniques described in Chapter 9 can hide one bit of information in a pixel. If a document uses the phrase "do not", it means that a "1" is being tagged, and if it uses a "don't" then it means that a "0" is being added as a tag.

If this process of flipping words is repeated throughout the document, then a larger amount of data can be hidden. Many of the techniques described in Chapter 10 can also be used effectively with text. Multiple word changes can be glued together to produce a serial number and their positions can be chosen to resist detection and protect the copyright holder.

The technique, unfortunately, requires a thorough understanding of spelling and grammar to succeed and it may be hard to automate with any great success. The easiest choices for words to flip or swap are the English contractions. For instance, "we are" and "we're" mean exactly the same thing. A program could easily identify all of the opportunities for word contraction and then embed a tag automatically by flipping the correct words to encode a particular pattern of bits.

I'm a small man.
—Anonymous,
Primary Colors.

Even this simple solution, however, is far from perfect. There are stylistic differences between the use of the complete phrase and the use of the contraction. Writers often make deliberate choices between the two. More formal prose aimed at more serious audiences may use the complete version, while casual prose, on the other hand, will almost always use the contraction. The king or queen of England, for instance, may sound strange and too familiar if they slip in a contraction, while a television comedian like Jay Leno might sound stiff if he used the complete form.

Mixing contractions and complete phrases could also muddle the rhythm of the piece. Most successful prose writers are carefully attuned to the rhythm formed from the emphasized and unemphasized syllables in words. A consistent beat strengthens the flow of the writing and makes it easier for the reader to absorb. Switching between the two forms deletes a syllable and may ruin the rhythm and consistency of the piece.

Synonyms

Another solution is to swap words that have the same meaning. The words "fine" and "nice" can often be used interchangeably and any swap would not destroy the rhythm of the sentence. These pairs, however, cannot be identified automatically because they might not always be indistinguishable. It may be acceptable to use either "We went walking on a fine day in June" or "We went walking on a nice day in June." But Carole King's song "One Fine Day" would sound wrong if it was titled "One Nice Day." Of course, the problem could be even greater because "fine" can describe the size of particles in a powder but "nice" has no meaning in this context.[1]

For all of these reasons, choosing word pairs automatically may not be practical. The best solution may be for the document's author

---

[1]What about a fine gneiss powder?

to identify pairs of words and let a computer do the job of producing the different versions of the document. The advantage of this solution is that the locations may be fairly random and not consistent so it will be difficult for someone to identify automatically the words being swapped. Contractions, on the other hand, are fairly obvious. The disadvantage is that a separate list of the swapped words must be kept. This acts like a key to the hidden tags and the tagging information can't be recovered without knowing the words being swapped.

Grammatical Choices

There are often many different ways of saying the same thing. That is, the same thing can be said many different ways. The phrasing of a sentence can also be flipped in the same way that different synonyms can be interchanged. In English, this process of changing sentence format may be easier to automate than the choice of synonyms because English grammar employs a relatively consistent pattern of nouns and verbs. Americans, in particular, enjoy the gradual precession of grammatic structure. In other languages, the rules of conjugation often change the endings of words when the words are used in different parts of the sentence and this may make it difficult to glue phrases together in random compositions.

Automated grammar checkers exist and often produce suggestions for correcting the sentence. In many cases, these suggestions are good and the technology could also be employed to embed tagging information automatically. But this solution offers some stylistic traps. Many writing style mongers continue to flog the advantages of "active voice" while moaning incessantly about the insidious effects of the "passive voice". Switching between the two is an easy way to write the same thing in different ways, but the two can have different effects. One may fit the current definition of grammatical correctness, while the other may be seen as a faux pas.

If this solution is used, it should be done with the supervision of the author.

Detecting Word Swaps

Anyone who tries to tamper with the tagging information produced by word flipping must identify which words changed. This is hardest when only one copy of the document can be found. In this case, it may be practically impossible to identify which words were candidates for word flipping. While some words may seem slightly wrong in the context, this could simply be the writer's choice, not the result of some synonym replacement algorithm.

Some approaches like contraction flipping and the introduction of spelling errors can be detected with only one copy of the document. A quick pass through the document can remove the contractions, clean up the spelling, and ensure that there are no weird details left in place.

The UNIX utility "diff" is a fairly sophisticated approach to identifying differences between files.

If someone has more than one copy of the document, then finding the changes is much easier. The two documents can be compared and any changes will stick out. A new hybrid of the documents can be produced by choosing between the two different versions. At each point there is a difference, a coin can be flipped. If it comes up heads, the word or phrase from document one is used in the hybrid. If it is tails, the version from document two is included. The tags in this hybrid will have little or no correlation with the two sources.

Chapter 10 describes several ways to use the position of the tags in a document to defend against someone who has multiple copies of a document. These solutions may be harder to use in this context because they need many more pairs of words or phrases to produce the same effect. If the number of potential documents to be tagged, however, is small, then it may still be manageable.

Mimic Functions

The process of swapping words or phrases is just a simple beginning and the approach can be generalized to a great degree. Instead of merely choosing between two words, a computer could make choices between different phrases and sentence structures. If this is done correctly, then the tagging data can be recovered successfully. The new complexity makes it harder to generate documents, but the result can be substantially more secure. There are reasons to believe that a well-constructed system can be as strong as, if not stronger than, encryption systems like RSA. Many people may not have a need for this level of security and it may not be practical in most cases, but the information is being included here to provide the foundation for future work and inspiration.

The basis for this approach is an abstraction concept known as a *grammar*. This is a more precise, mathematical definition of the rules of composition taught in school. Some linguistic scientists like Noam Chomsky used the form to describe how humans make sense out of words. The abstraction was also adopted by computer scientists, who used it for the model for building programming languages.

In the most abstract sense, a grammar consists of:

Terminals In reality, these are all the words and phrases that make up a language. They're called terminals because the process of creating a sentence stops when it consists of all of these. The terminals are represented with ordinary type when they're used in examples.

Variables These are used to describe how the grammar works. They will be shown in **boldface**. For instance, a simple grammar has two variables: **noun** and **verb**.

Productions These are rules that replace a variable with another collection of variables and terminals. For instance, a simple grammar might enclose two different nouns and the production might be indicated like this: **noun** → Bob ‖ Mary Jane. That is, the variable, **noun** can be replaced by either the terminal "Bob" or the terminal phrase "Mary Jane". The vertical lines indicate that there is an equal choice between the two.

The collection of all three parts creates a grammar. One of the most common forms is the *context-free grammar*, which has only productions that have one variable on the left-hand side. *Context-sensitive grammars*, on the other hand, allow productions to replace variables only in certain contexts. Most of computer science research focuses on context-free grammars because they are the easiest to understand and use to write algorithms that solve problems. Here's a simple context-free grammar:

Start	→	**noun** **verb**
noun	→	Bob ‖ Ray
verb	→	ate dinner. ‖ flew to France.

The grammar can produce sentences like "Bob flew to France" or "Ray ate dinner." In fact, there are four different possible sentences that can be produced from the initial variable, **Start**. The process of taking apart a sentence from a grammar and determining the sequences of productions that lead to it is known as *parsing*. This is similar to diagramming sentences.

Information tags can be produced with grammars by using the data from the tag to choose between productions. In the last example, there are two choices for a noun and two choices for a verb. One bit of information could make the first choice and the second bit of information could make the second choice. The information could be recovered by reversing the process. Here's an example:

Start	→	**nounverb**
noun	→	Bob ‖ Ray
verb	→	fished **where** ‖ bowled **where**
where	→	in **direction** Iowa. ‖ in **direction** Ohio.
direction	→	northern ‖ southern

Step	Answer in Progress	Bit Hidden	Production Choice
1	**Start**	*none*	**Start → noun verb**
2	**noun verb**	1	**noun→ Ray**
3	Ray **verb**	0	**verb → fished where**
4	Ray fished **where**	1	**where → in direction Ohio.**
5	Ray fished in **direction** Ohio.	0	**direction → northern**

This example is not more complicated than the word swapping example at the beginning of the chapter. In fact, it is equivalent. More complicated grammars, however, can produce very different results. Here's another example:

Start	→	**noun verb**
noun	→	Bob ‖ Ray
verb	→	ate dinner **modifier**. ‖ flew to **where**.
where	→	France ‖ Egypt ‖ Russia ‖ Japan
modifier	→	by candlelight in **where2** ‖
		at a restaurant in **where2**
where2	→	Moscow ‖ Tokyo ‖ London ‖ Paris

In this example, the flights can only go to countries while the dinners are eaten in cities. That is, one sentence produced by this grammar is "Bob ate dinner at a restaurant in Moscow" while another reads "Bob flew to France." The choice of the words late in the sentence depends upon the words chosen at the beginning of the sentence. This effect is the basis for all of the security because it makes it hard if not impossible for a computer to try and correlate the differences between sentences.

Grammars can grow arbitrarily complex if someone tries to encapsulate complicated facts and details. Some grammars are easier to parse than others. Some of the easiest to parse are in *Greibach normal form*, which means that the phrases on the right side of the production have the terminals at the beginning and the variables at the end.

Grammars can also be ambiguous if two different sequences of productions can lead to the same sentence. This may not be important in many situations, but it can have dramatic effects on the process of hiding information in text. The sequence of productions determines the tagging bits that are stored away. If two different sequences could have generated the same sentence, then the correct tagging data can't be recovered. Ensuring that a grammar is not ambiguous is relatively easy to do if the grammar is in Greibach normal form. If every phrase on the right-hand side of a production has a slightly different sequence of terminals at the beginning, then the entire grammar is non-ambiguous. There are also non-ambiguous grammars that don't fit this definition, but the process of using them lies outside the scope of the book.

Parsing is beyond the scope of this book. All of the books on compilers give the subject plenty of discussion. Parsing context-free grammars in Greibach normal form is easy to do. The output file of sentences is processed from beginning to end. At each step, there is only one set of productions in question. The words at the start of the file are compared with the terminals in the productions. The choice of which production was used should be obvious.

If the grammars are in another format, then the process can be more complicated. The most general parsing algorithm for context-free grammars [HU79] is relatively slow, but it can handle any context-free grammar in any form. If the grammars are not context free, then the question is more complicated and parsing may be very inefficient for computers to do automatically. The details of this process are a topic of much study in academic computer science and it would be both impossible and inefficient to give the topic the discussion it deserves right here.

Making Choices

Grammars do not need to have only two choices. In most of the short examples, there were only two choices between the different productions and it was easy to connect one choice with a zero and the other with a one. There may be many choices and it is not simple to map *n* choices to bits. The problem is that the connection between the information bits in the tag and the choices must be one to one so it can be reversed to recover the information.

The solution is to build a tree with two choices that is much like the tree used for Huffman coding. That algorithm also arranges for a one-to-one relationship between characters and bits. The Huffman construction algorithm is described in the section beginning on page 44.

Figure 8.1 shows a balanced tree that can construct the one to one connection between the four choices for a city and the information bits that are being hidden by the process. The bits "00" would be hidden implicitly by the choice of "London" and "01" by the choice of "Moscow". A different tree would be constructed for each variable and the choices of its productions.

The Huffman algorithm will weight the choices of the individual characters to try and approximate the frequency with which they are found in a source file. Figure 8.1 shows an equally weighted tree, but this won't always be the case. Figure 8.2 shows a tree constructed to make choices between six different cities. This tree cannot be equally weighted and so some cities represent three bits of tagging information and some represent only two.

The tree shown here affects the structure of the final sentences generated from a grammar during the process of hiding the tagging bits. In Figure 8.1, each city will occur in a sentence 25% of the time because the tree is equally weighted. In the case represented by Figure 8.2, only London and Moscow will appear 25% of the time each. The other four cities will each appear 12.5% of the time.

This distribution is based upon the assumption that the tagging bits will be zero as often as they are one. This may not be the case in

This scheme is also used in Figure 10.3 to make dithering choices.

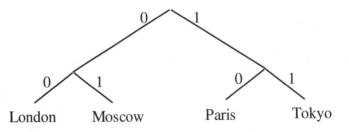

Figure 8.1. A tree designed to make the choices between four cities with equal weight. The tagging information of "01" is hidden by the choice of Moscow.

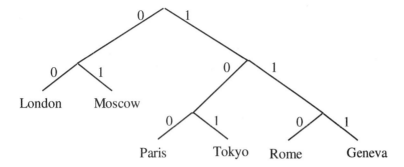

Figure 8.2. Here is an unequally weighted tree produced to make choices between six different cities that might be used for a location. The tagging information of "01" is still hidden by the choice of Moscow, but "110" is the binary name of the Rome in this case.

practice. If pure ASCII text is used as the tagging information, then zeros are more common than ones in standard text. This will skew the choice of productions in the final sentences and may offer some weakness for an attacker to exploit. One solution is to compress the tagging information. This process decreases the entropy and makes each bit pattern more equally likely to appear.

An Example

Several years ago, I built a grammar-based system to test the feasibility and prove that the system was workable. The software was written in Pascal and converted to C by D. Jason Penney. Any U.S. citizen residing in the United States can have a free copy of the software by asking me (mail to pcw@access.digex.net) and promising not to export it. While I have never submitted the software to the Department of Commerce to determine whether it is covered by the rules about exporting munitions, I can only assume that it is covered. If anyone wants to go through the trouble of making an application, you're welcome to try.

The software can accept any grammar in Greibach normal form. The input format was fairly straightforward. Each variable must begin with an asterisk in order to distinguish it from a terminal word. The productions start with the name of the variable and the choices are separated by slashes ("/"). There is an option for weighting the choices by adding a constant after the slash. In the example that follows, this option is effectively turned off by always using the value ".1".

Here's a small part of the grammar used to encode information in a text that simulates the voice-over of a baseball game. Although it is not apparent from this fragment, the text has the right number of outs per inning and the right number of innings per game. It doesn't, however, keep track of the score or arrange for the game to go into extra innings if the score is tied. This is a limitation of using context-free grammars. They always produce the same text from a variable no matter what the context (i.e., score). A more complicated system could avoid this problem.

```
*BlogsInfieldHit = He tries to bunt, and
                   *WhapperInfielder
                   *BuntResponseHit /.1/
        He knocks it down the line
        between the legs of
         *WhapperInfielder *period /.1/
        He lifts it over the head of
        *WhapperInfielder *HitResult /.1/
        The batter gets a piece of
        it *HitResult /.1/
        Nice job *HitResult /.1/
        Great hit *HitResult /.1/
        It's contact time  *HitResult /.1/
        Nice hit *HitResult /.1/
        He waps it into the shortstop's glove,
        but he can't control it .
        Safe at first . /.1/
        Whoa ! That swing was on the
        money *HitResult /.1/
        Super looper for a hit /.1/
        He knocks a line-drive into the head of
        *WhapperInfielder /.05//
*BlogsInfieldOut =
        He grounds out to *WhapperInfielder
        *period/.1/
        He  knocks a line-drive into
        the glove of *WhapperInfielder /.1/
        He tries to bunt, and
```

```
        *WhapperInfielder *BuntResponseOut /.1/
    He knocks an easy bouncer to
        *WhapperInfielder *period /.1/
    He  pops it up to *WhapperInfielder
    *period/.1/
    He  bounces one off the ground into the
        first-baseman's glove ./ .1//
*EndOfInning =
    Well, that's the end of their chances in
    this inning, *Announcer *period
    *Commercial/.1/
    No more at bats left in this inning.
    *Commercial /.1/
    The inning's over .
    Some kind of ballplayer, huh,
        *Announcer *period *Commercial /.1/
    Yowza! End of the inning . Hard to imagine
        life without baseball? Right, *Announcer
        *questionmark *Commercial /.1/
    That inning proves why baseball is
        the nation's game . *Commercial /.1//
*Return = Back to the game,
    *Announcer *period /.1/
    We now return to the game between
    the Blogs and the Whappers . /.1/
    Now back to the game . /.1/
    Just wanted to say thanks to
    our sponsors for those great messages . /.1//
*Commercial = This is WZZZ-TV bringing you
    the ballgame!  *BeerCom *BeerCom
    *CarCom *Return/.1/
    We're here at WZZZ-TV bringing
    you the ballgame!
    *CarCom *CarCom *BeerCom *Return /.1/
    This is the WZZZ baseball network!
    *BeerCom *CarCom *CarCom
    *BeerCom *BeerCom *Return /.1/
    Now a message from our sponsors.
    *BeerCom *BeerCom *BeerCom *Return /.1/
    Now a very special message from our sponsors.
```

```
        *CarCom *BeerCom  *CarCom *Return /.1//
*BeerOne = Imported Name . / .1/
          Imported Label ./.1/
          Imported Aura . /.1/
          Imported Concept ./.1/
          Imported Danger Warning in
          German . /.1//
*BeerTwo = American Taste . /.1/
          American Flavor . /.1/
          Clean American Taste ./.1/
          No Overly-flavorful
          Assault on your tongue . /.1//
*BeerThree = fermentation is natural ? /.1/
          yeast is one of Mother Nature's
          Creatures ? /.1/
          yeast is a beast of Nature ? /.1/
          beer is natural ? /.1//
*BeerFour = Support Mother Nature
            and drink. /.1/
        Go green and support
        the environment . /.1/
        Support Natural Things and
        drink another ! /.1/
        Live a natural life and
        drink some more ! /.1//
*BeerCom = St. Belch . *BeerOne *BeerTwo /.1/
        Longing for adventure ?
        Open a bottle of St. Belch ! /.1/
        Did you know that *BeerThree *BeerFour /.1/
        Hey! *BeerFour /.1/
        Man comes up to Bob on the street and says,
        ''Want a St. Belch ?" and his
        friend says, "Sure, I'm a man and I
        love to drink ." It turns out the
        Man was the head of a Fortune 500
        company looking for a new Chairman
        of the Board of Directors . He
        hires Bob for $350,000 a year . /.1/
        St. Belch Beer: Especially tailored
        for men who watch ballgames . /.1//
```

Figure 8.3 shows the output from an extensive grammar developed to mimic the voice-over from a baseball game. The figure shows only the first part of a 26k file generated from hiding this quote:

I then told her the key-word which belonged to no language and saw her surprise. She told me that it was impossible for she believed herself the only possessor of that word which she kept in her memory and which she never wrote down... This disclosure fettered Madame d'Urfé to me. That day I became the master of her soul and I abused my power. —*Casanova, 1757, as quoted by David Kahn in* **The Codebreakers**.

Turning a short bit of text into a long text is one of the inherent problems with the grammar-based system. Each choice can include only several bits of data.

```
Well Bob, Welcome to yet another game between the Whappers
and the Blogs here in scenic downtown Blovonia. I think it is
fair to say that there is plenty of BlogFever brewing in the
stands as the hometown comes out to root for its favorites.
The Umpire throws out the ball. Top of the inning. No outs
yet for the Whappers. Here we go. Jerry Johnstone adjusts the
cup and enters the batter's box. Here's the pitch. Nothing
on that one. Here comes the pitch It's a curvaceous beauty.
He just watched it go by. And the next pitch is a smoking gun.
He lifts it over the head of Harrison "Harry" Hanihan for a
double! Yup. What a game so far today. Now, Mark Cloud adjusts
the cup and enters the batter's box. Yeah. He's winding up.
What looks like a spitball. He swings for the stands, but
no contact. It's a rattler. He just watched it go by. He's
winding up. What a blazing comet. Swings and misses ! Strike
out. He's swinging at the umpire. The umpire reconsiders
until the security guards arrive. Yup, got to love this
stadium.
```

Figure 8.3. Some text produced from the baseball context-free grammar on page 112.

Using Grammars

The process of creating grammars to describe simple sentences is not
hard, but it is quite labor intensive. At first glance, most people will
not want to go through all of this work to mark a document in a secure
way. The writer must do more than simply generate one sentence to
describe what is going on. A grammar can illustrate many different
ways of saying the same thing. The only ancillary benefit to the writer
may be clarity of thought. A diagrammed sentence is cleaner and often
better.

There are secondary places, however, where grammars may prove
useful. Many documents have background information that is not an
important part of the document. For instance, many television dramas
show people walking through the mall, often accompanied by the type
of soft, inoffensive music found in these places. The words to these
songs may not be important to the plot, so they may be generated by
some grammar system.

A grammar system may be useful in generating common messages
that are repeated constantly. Many residents of New York City grew
tired of the new recorded messages played in cabs reminding them to
take all of their valuables. The messages said the same thing each day
and the sound quickly wore a groove in the brains of the residents
who rode in the cabs often. If the messages were generated from a
selection of grammars, they could change often.

Assessing the Security of Grammar

The grammar-based systems for changing and swapping words may
offer some of the best security around. If people are able to assemble a
collection of documents that were marked with different tagging bits,
they still may not be able to determine the structure of the grammar
enough to have their will with the machine.

Measuring the security of the system is difficult to do because
many assumptions must be made to create a model of how the system
encodes information in the word choices and how an attacker may try
and learn enough about the grammars to try and tamper with the tags.
In the PAC model defined by Les Valiant [Val84], attackers can look
at many random productions by the grammar and also generate their
own sentences and ask whether they belong to the grammar. Given
these conditions, Michael Kearns and Les Valient show that "learn-

ing" Boolean formulae, finite automata, or constant-depth threshold circuits is at least as difficult as inverting RSA encryption or factoring Blum integers (x, such that $x = pq$, p, q are prime, and $p, q = 3 \ mod \ 4$) [KV89, Kea89].

Dana Angluin and Michael Kharitonov [AK91] extended the work of Kearns and Valiant as well as the work of Moni Naor and M. Yung [NY89, NY90]. They showed that it wasn't possible to predict membership in a class defined by a context-free grammar—at least using any known efficient algorithms.

This means that it can be just as hard to learn enough about text generated from a grammar as it is to break RSA encryption. The rub in this argument, however, is the word "can". The depth of the problem depends upon the grammar itself and there are no simple guidelines on how to create such a difficult grammar. My earlier book, *Disappearing Cryptography*, goes into greater detail on how to construct grammar-based systems and shows several ways that grammars can be modified automatically to increase their complexity. This is a good source to begin exploring the matter in more detail.

There is no reason why the grammars can't be generated automatically from an analysis of the writing. This is an open problem for the reader. Some of the work done in automatic translation and grammar checking may make a good beginning.

Summary

Changing the actual words of a text document is an interesting method for tagging it. The main advantage is that the information is part of the document and it is not easy to either detect it or remove it. The algorithms from Chapter 7 do not alter the content of the text, but the tagging information can be stripped away if the text is scanned into a computer via optical character recognition or reformatted.

The biggest problem with the algorithms in this chapter is the amount of work necessary to modify the words. Simple synonyms can be substituted fairly automatically, but they still the need the approval of the writer to prevent inadvertent embarrassment. The grammar-based methods at the end of the chapter are much more secure, but they require even more work. The author must produce some grammar that offers many different ways of saying the same thing.

Automatic methods for constructing grammars are an interesting challenge. There are certainly programs that can analyze text and establish some sort of context-free grammar that models the flow of the language. But it is not clear whether it is possible to maintain the meaning of the language.

Chapter 9

Pixel Modification

Images can be tagged with data by fiddling with the information contained in a pixel. This chapter addresses the different approaches for hiding a bit or two of information in a pixel. Chapter 10 shows how to knit these together to store more data.

Lipstick Colors

Here is an excerpt from the catalog of **Color Squared**, *a makeup company aiming at delivering the young women in science a set of colors they can call their own. The company is targeting this group of serious women who may not have their fashion needs served by older companies that still aim their products at those Cosmopolitan girls. Here are their deep red lipstick colors for next season:*

Iceland Lava When a new volcano explodes, *ex nihilo*, out of the ocean we can only celebrate and cerebrate. Feel like Venus herself emerging in this basalt-laden new color that evokes the red hot magma breaking the surface of the ocean.

Ring of Fire We embrace the serious attitude of Mr. Johnny Cash *and* the majestic power of the volcanic action lacing the Pacific Rim where the natives quickly learned the fury of volcanoes scorned. Apply this smoldering tincture to your lips to send a message that says "sacrifice me".

Subduction Zone Evoke the deep, hidden regions of your soul by wearing the burning color of the earth's crust returning to the mantle. Watch him melt into you like the Pacific plate being delivered to the center of the earth by the majesty and shear mass of the Andes mountains.

Jurassic Blood Capture the mystery and passionate debate about the metabolism of the dinosaurs with this deep red, oxygen-laden salve. Let him wonder whether you're filled with hot-blooded rapture of the vernal equinox or the scheming sang froid of the feline/prey dyad.

Adding Data to Pixels

Images are one of the best places to include individualized tags because the files are large and often filled with some noise. This chapter will cover different ways that information can be packed into an individual pixel. Often, this may be as little as one bit of data. This may not seem like much, but Chapter 10 describes how to group together multiple pixels to store enough data to leave a meaningful tag. This can be a substantial amount of information when all of the pixels are used. Some image files take more than a megabyte of data and if one eighth can be devoted to pixel encoding schemes, then that's more than 120k of data.

The process of modifying image files is not particularly hard, but it may often include subtle details. In many cases, different file formats and compression schemes have already claimed much of the noise. In other cases, some ways of modifying the image stand out more than others. None of the schemes are perfect, but they can produce very good results.

The schemes involve changing the color an insignificant amount. What qualifies as "insignificant" is a large part of the problem. A large change in a grainy image of, say, an acne-scarred alien will be much less obvious than a small change in a very simple image filled with pure colors like the Japanese flag. Determining the amount to change an image is the greatest part of the problem.

Chapter 4 discusses some of the ways to identify the amount of noise in an image by using the compression algorithms like JPEG. These compression algorithms are lossy, so they try to construct a simple model of the image that comes close to the actual one. Extremely fine detail is often lost and new detail that is filled with tagging data can be put in its place.

But even a small change in a pixel may alert attentive people looking for tags. If the selection of colors in an image includes many pairs of colors that are imperceptibly close to each other, then there is a good chance that someone modified the image to include some tags.

The rest of this chapter will discuss several schemes for modifying pixels to include information without tipping off anyone to the presence of the hidden data. The schemes are tuned to various file formats that are common for storing images.

Least Significant Bits

The simplest approach to encoding information is to modify the intensity of each pixel by a small amount. This is easy to do, however, only when the file containing the image is set up to contain the complete bitmap in all detail. This is often true for black and white images, but usually a luxury for color images. Representing a black and white image with a byte per pixel gives each pixel 256 gray levels—a system that is simple, relatively compact, and in tune with the architectural requirements of general CPUs that move data one byte at a time.

Color images, on the other hand, are best represented by 24-bit color. One byte represents the amount of red in the image, another the amount of blue, and the third the amount of green. Other alternatives also use 24 bits to measure the amount of cyan, magenta, and yellow in a pixel. In many cases, the computers actually use 32 bits for each pixel and use the fourth byte for an *alpha channel* that measures the transparency of the pixel or some other quality of that point. Most modern, circa 1996 CPUs move data in 32-bit blocks and it can be significantly faster to use more bits per pixel.

There are also many compromises. Black and white images may include only 16 levels of gray if each pixel is represented by 4 bits. Color images can use only 16 bits per pixel if the number of bits allocated to each color is smaller. One popular solution is to give 6 bits to red, 6 bits to green, and 4 bits to blue. In each of these cases, modification of the individual pixel is still easy because the color intensities are still stored at each pixel.

The problems occur when even more efficiency is needed. Many people use more compact data formats to save space while storing images. A common solution is to choose 256 colors that are as close as

The least significant bit in a binary number is like the least significant digit in a decimal number, i.e., the rightmost. If the number is 300,029, then the least significant digit is 9. Computers represent numbers in base 2 or binary so the least significant value is a bit that is either 0 or 1.

possible to the colors in the image and store them in a table. Each pixel uses one byte to choose a color from the table instead of representing the RGB colors directly. The GIF format is one example of this approach. In many cases, the limitations of computer architecture force this on people. Building a video display hardware that maintains a color lookup table and uses one byte per pixel is significantly cheaper than building one that uses 24 or 32 bits per pixel. If the image is stored with color tables, then the next section beginning on page 126 describes how to modify the pixels.

When the image is stored with the intensities available, then it is easy to modify the intensity by a small amount. The simplest solution is to flip the *least significant bit* to match the data to be stored at the pixel. If the image is a 24-bit color image, then three bits can be stored by modifying the least significant bits of the red, blue, and green intensities.

In many cases, the least significant bits are simple to modify without changing the look of the image. Many least significant bits are close to random. Figure 9.1 shows a black and white image and Figure 9.2 shows the least significant bits. Except where the image is washed out,

Figure 9.1. An image of the author's office scanned from a color film print and converted into a gray-scale image. The half-toning in this image was accomplished by the PostScript printing process.

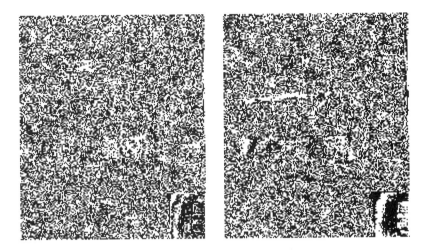

Figure 9.2. The least significant bits of Figure 9.1 are on the left. The next to least significant bits are on the right. Both appear random except at the most washed-out places.

the patterns look close to random. The randomness extends deeper. The right side of Figure 9.2 shows the next to least significant bit plane. There is still a fair amount of randomness.

If the image is fairly random and more room for tagging data is required, then the two or three least significant bits may all be replaced with the tagging data. Using more and more bits increases the degradation of the image. Changing the least significant bit will change the intensity at that pixel by only 1 unit. Changing the next to least significant bit will change the intensity by 2 units. Changing the next bit will modify it by 4 units. If all are flipped together, then there is the potential that a pixel will change by 7 units. This is only about 2.5% if the intensities range between 0 and 255.

The average change of a pixel can be much smaller. Fifty percent of the pixels will not change when tagging data replaces the least significant bit—if both the new and the old data are fairly random and well distributed. 25% increase by one unit and 25% decrease by one unit.

If the two least significant bits are replaced by tagging data, then the math gets more complicated. $\frac{1}{16}$ of the bits will change by +3, $\frac{1}{8}$ by +2, $\frac{3}{16}$ by +1, $\frac{1}{4}$ by 0, $\frac{3}{16}$ by −1, $\frac{1}{8}$ by −2, and $\frac{1}{16}$ by −3. The average change will be only ±1.25.

Understanding the Randomness

The source of the randomness depends upon the provenance of the image. These images came from a print of a film negative that was scanned in by a flatbed scanner. In many cases, the intensity of a particular pixel is governed by random physical processes. The digitized image is made by photons hitting arrays of light-sensitive CCDs (charge-coupled devices). The number of photons is fairly random and the number hitting a particular part of a CCD array may be quite small when the light levels are low. The randomness in the least significant bit often emerges from this effect.

Some of the best sources of digitized photos can remove large amounts of this randomness. The best digital cameras are tested in a lab, so the sensitivity of each pixel in the CCD array is known in advance. This sensitivity profile can be used to calibrate the camera and correct any errors introduced by the relative differences in each pixel. NASA uses this when they build CCD arrays for space.

Other amounts of randomness emerge from digitization. Each pixel in the final image is really an average of all the details cov-

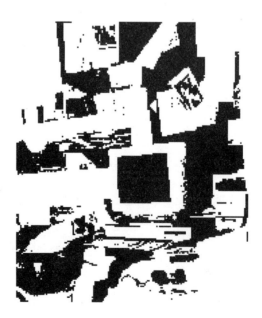

Figure 9.3. These are the most significant bits of the photo in Figure 9.1. The seven least significant bits were deleted to contrast the images in Figure 9.2.

ered by that pixel. When the pixels are small and the details are large, then this often has little effect. A picture of a clear, blue winter sky will have plenty of blue and each pixel should be close to the same color. But when the pixels cover a large amount of small detail, then they contain the average color of all of these items. A digitized image of a wheat field may portray billions of grains with thousands of pixels. Each pixel is a average of a bit of dark soil, some stalk, some grain, and maybe some bugs. At this level of detail, some amount of the randomness comes from the fact that each pixel represents a different collection of things.

Still other randomness in the image comes from the lens. Photographs are close enough to the view we see from our eyes that we often forget that they are really two-dimensional projections of a three-dimensional realm. In most cases, the images are very complicated projections produced by a clear lens with a complicated profile. The lens was designed to produce an image that is ideal in some sense, but it is still quite different from a perfect reflection of reality.

One intriguing effect is prismatic. A lens will bend light of different wavelengths a different amount. The lenses are designed to minimize this effect, but they can't remove it. The effects are visible along the edges of objects when the blue light is shifted a different amount than the red light. A purple object may appear bluer along one edge and redder along another.

The effects of a lens are beyond the scope of this book. Optical design is a highly advanced field that depends on a significant amount of computational power. The path of each ray of light through the lens can be studied and quantified to predict the effects of the lens upon the image. Highly advanced packages are available to study this effect.

Fake Randomness

The greatest danger is that the randomness may not be random enough. Although it may look random to the naked eye, there may be a computer model that describes the least significant bits across the image. If this model can be used to predict how the least significant bits should behave, then it could reveal the existence of the tagging data and maybe even the data itself.

The creation of these models is not a simple process and I don't know of any easy way to do it. But there is no reason why someone with a firm understanding of the physics of image creation can't use this to determine when and even how much the least significant bits of an image may be changed. The structure of randomness is one of the weaknesses of this approach, but it is not clear how easy it will be for someone to exploit it.

Color Table Quandaries

Most color images on the Internet use color tables to shrink the size of the image. Each pixel is represented by a small number of bits that point to an entry in a color table that gives the true red, green, and blue intensities for the pixel. The simple trick of flipping the least significant bits of these pixels can produce glaring errors. For instance, one pixel may contain color 30, which is purple. Changing the least significant bit to make the color 31 could pull up an entirely different color, perhaps white. Clearly, this approach could destroy the image and make it look like noise.

These images can still contain tagging data, but the system must be approached with more finesse and attention to detail. If the algorithms are sensitive to the color values of the pixel, then that approach can still work. None of these solutions are perfect, but they are often quite serviceable.

Sorting the Color Table

The simplest approach is to sort the color table. The color table consists of triples: $c_i = (r_i, g_i, b_i)$. If the table is sorted, the colors with the closest red values will be next to each other in the table. Among the colors with similar red values, the ones with the closest green will be near each other. Finally, among the colors with similar red and green values, those with a similar blue intensity will be next to each other.

The attraction of this approach is clear. Changing the least significant bit will often change between similar colors. If the color table is random, which it often is, a change in the smallest bit could change between colors on opposite ends of the spectrum. But when it is sorted, the change will be minimized. It is also possible to sort the color table using either the blue or the green intensities as the most significant part of the sorting algorithm.

There are limitations to this approach. First, simple sorting puts too much emphasis on one of the three intensity values. For instance, here's a sorted sequence of RGB triples: (127,58,95), (127,240,32), (128,53,93). The first and third colors are quite close to each other while second one is significantly different despite the fact that they are in correctly sorted order. Some solutions to minimizing this solution can be found in the next section.

The second problem is that jumps in the table may still exist. Here's another list of four colors: (12,80,92), (14,92,52), (16,85,77), (80,102,44). If this was a 2-bit color table, then the four colors would be represented by the binary numbers: 00, 01, 10, and 11, respectively. Changing the least significant bit of a pixel that held either 00 or 01 would switch between the colors (12,80,92) and (14,92,52), but changing the least significant bit of a pixel holding 10 or 11 would flip between (16,85,77) and (80,102,44).

The second problem can be mitigated by smoothing the effects of the color table. If two very different colors are only one significant bit apart, then one can be discarded and replaced with a similar one. The problem is determining which one. The later sections of this chapter describe how to create new color tables that do a good job of approximating an existing one. If there are n colors in a table to be sorted, then a new table with $\frac{n}{2}$ colors can be created. This table can be used to determine the most important colors to be kept. This guide can be used to remove the nearby colors.

In any case, the solution can be hidden by adding an additional permutation. The colors can be sorted, the data can be included by flipping the least significant bits, and then the colors can be rescrambled or returned to their original position. This obscures the use of the sorting solution without inconveniencing anyone trying to recover the tag. Anyone searching for the tagging data can sort the color table again to determine the correct least significant bits at a pixel. If sorting is used, the rescrambling is an ideal solution.

The section beginning on page 132 describes how to scramble the color table to encode a value.

Smarter Sorting

Sorting color triplets cannot be done perfectly, but there are better ways to approach the problem. One solution is to convert the RGB colors into another popular color representation system often called HSV, which is an acronym for the three values in the triplet: hue, saturation, and value.

The *hue* chooses a number that represents the position along the spectrum between red and violet. The red values are the lowest numbers and the numbers increase through the spectrum of orange, yellow, blue, indigo, and finally violet. The *saturation* determines how much of the hue is available. A heavily saturated blue, for instance, would be all blue without other colors mixed in. A lightly saturated color would include other components and be closer to gray. The *value* is the amount of light. Large-valued colors are close to white. Low-valued colors are close to black. Basic colors have about 50% of the value.

If the RGB or CMY colors are converted into HSV values, then the sorting is going to do a better job placing similar hues next to each other. The danger is now that similar hues may have significantly different amounts of saturation or value. The best solution may be to sort first on value, then on saturation, and finally on hue.

Another approach is to use a more sophisticated algorithm for "sorting" the table. The problem is not really a problem in sorting, and this is why the approach often fails. The problem is finding the best way to arrange points in three dimensions along a one-dimensional line so that the points that are closest in 3D are also closest in this 1D world. This is more a problem of multi-dimensional geometry than simple sorting.

See page 177 for a description of how Romana Machado's EzStego program sorts the color palette using a variation of the traveling salesman's problem.

Creating Smaller Color Tables

Taking an image with a large number of colors and finding the best set of colors for a table is a common problem in computer graphics. Many machines can display only 256 colors because they use only one byte for each pixel. Images must constantly be displayed by converting them.

The problem is useful for tagging applications because it makes it possible to introduce small changes into each pixel without changing the look of the image. If there are 256 colors in an image, then the color reduction algorithm could be used to find 128 basic colors that do a good job approximating the 256 colors. Then, a new color table could be created out of identical pairs of the 128 colors. That is, colors 0 and 1 would be the same, 2 and 3 would be the same, 4 and 5, etc. If the least significant bit of any pixel was changed, the image would not look different because the color wouldn't change.

Choosing a good set of colors is something of an art as well as a mathematical science. Many readers may have different opinions of the best approach to creating a smaller set of colors and this book will not attempt to make any strong argument for one approach or another. If such a set can be created, then information can be hidden by twiddling the least significant bit.

Here's a simple algorithm that works by clumping the colors together until the number of clumps matches the desired number of colors. Imagine there are n colors, $\{c_1, \ldots, c_n\}$, and $D(c_i)$ produces the color that is closest. $\delta(c_i, c_j)$ measures the distance. There are many different possible distance functions, but the simplest sum up the absolute values of the differences between the red, green, and blue intensities. More sophisticated functions may square the differences or weight some color higher than another because of the reaction of the human eye.

The algorithm is straightforward. First a table consisting of the values of the $D(c_i)$ is constructed for all c_i. If the number of colors is small, then this may be done by brute force. If the number is larger, then a three-dimensional sweeping plane algorithm can be used. Computing the three-dimensional Delaunay triangulation will join each point in space with all of its nearest neighbors. This can be converted into the values of $\delta(c_i)$ by examining each point in turn.

The rest of the algorithm consists of finding the shortest distance between two colors and then clumping them together until the desired number of clumps is left. The result is a good approximation of the colors. The representative color for each clump can be chosen by averaging the colors in the clump. This representative nature works well in tight clumps, but it can be a dismal failure when the clumps include disparate colors. The average may look like none of the colors in the group.

This solution will produce a reasonable approximation of the colors in the image. The one problem with it is that very different colors gain significant weight. For instance, a picture with many different shades of blue may get all of the blues reduced to one color, effectively wiping out the subtle shading.

Better Color Reduction

One of the more sophisticated packages for hiding information in the least significant bits is the S-Tools software from Andrew Brown. The software uses a color reduction algorithm from Paul Heckbert's bachelor's thesis. [Hec82] This algorithm breaks up the three-dimensional color space into boxes instead of clumping like colors together in the hope of avoiding the problems produced by averaging the colors in the clumps.

Heckbert argues that the difference between these solutions is akin to the difference between the two halves of the United Congress. The House of Representatives provides equal representation based upon population, while the Senate provides equal representation based upon area. The clumping algorithm is equivalent to the House, while Heckbert's algorithm works along the lines of the Senate.

The Heckbert algorithm begins with a three-dimensional box that is 256 units by 256 units by 256 units. This box will be subdivided until there is one box for each one of the desired colors, i.e., 128, 256. At the end, one color is chosen for each box by either finding the center of the box or averaging the pixels in the box.

Here's the subdivision algorithm:

1. Make one box and place all of the colors in it.

2. Repeat this step until there are n boxes that will represent the final n colors.

    (a) For each box, compute the minimum and maximum value for each dimension. That is, find the smallest and largest value of red for any color in the box, the smallest and largest value of green, and the smallest and largest value of blue.

    (b) For each dimension of each box, measure the difference between the minimum and maximum color. This might be the difference in absolute length or it might be the difference in luminosity.

    (c) Find the greatest difference in all of the boxes and split this particular box along this dimension. Heckbert suggests this can be done by either finding the median color in the box along this dimension or simply choosing the geometric middle. This breaks the box in half.

3. Choose a representative color for all of the original colors in each box. S-Tools offers three choices: center of the box, average of the colors, or average of the pixels.

The subdivision algorithm resists clumping different colors together because it always splits the box with the greatest range of one color.

Choosing Colors

The simplest approach to using a color table and mixing in data is to cut the color table in half and use each color twice. This solution, however, is not particularly innocent. Many color image formats permit a flexible number of bits per pixel. If there are only 128 colors needed, then the image would save space by allocating only seven bits to each pixel not eight. A color table with 128 different colors repeated twice would seem suspicious.

The S-Tools system produced by Andrew Brown uses a repetitive approximation. First, it starts out reducing the 256 colors to, say, 64 colors. Then it goes through the process of adding information to each pixel in the standard way for a 24-bit color image. That means the least significant bit of the red, blue, and green bytes is replaced by the tagging data.

The problem is that each of the 64 colors in the image could be permuted into one of 7 similar colors. Not all of the 7×64 colors will be added to the image. Some colors in the image may be used rarely. If only one pixel uses that color, then the old color will be replaced by the new color produced by twiddling the least significant bits. If only a small number of pixels use the color, then only a small number of new colors may be produced. Some of them will probably be the same.

S-Tools goes through a limbo process. First it reduces the colors. Then it permutes the pixels and counts the number of colors now in the image. If there is less than the desired number, say 255, then it stops. Otherwise, it begins again and reduces the number of colors to be even smaller. It continues repeating this process until the final number of colors is under the limit.

This process can produce some nice results that are subtly shaded and smooth. The final color table is less suspicious, but it still can stand out. The colors will generally fall into constellations that are separated by one bit. The most common colors will have eight colors in their group and the eight colors will be arranged in a cube produced by changing the least significant bits of one color. These constellations should stand out to someone looking for any tagging bits or watermarks.

A more sophisticated process might choose permutation inside the box. S-Tools chooses a central color to represent the box first, then it permutes this color by changing the least significant bits. All of the colors produced differ by only the least significant bits. A better solution may change the color by a large amount if the box is bigger. If the box is eight units long in each direction, then the color might be changed by four units.

Permuting the Color Table

If images come with a color table, then tagging information can be hidden in the color table. There is no reason why the colors need to be in the table in any particular order, so the order can be changed to hide an identifying tag. Each person could get an image that was exactly the same, but the order of the colors in the table would reveal the serial number of the image.

There is a wide variety of different schemes for converting the order of values in a color table into a number. The simplest solution may be to view the color table as a permutation. A color table sorted according to, say, RGB values would be the basis. All other tables would be permutations of that.

Identifying the permutation must be done in a unique way. First, sort the colors in order: $c_1 \ldots c_n$. Let $p_t(c_i)$ stand for the position of color c_i after step t. At time $t = 0$, $p_0(c_i) = i$. Later, colors will be removed from the list and the positions will change. For instance, imagine at step 1, color c_2 was removed from the list. At that point $p_1(c_1) = 1$ but $p_i(c_i) = i - 1$ for all $i > 2$.

Now imagine a particular color table: $d_1 \ldots d_n$. Let $P_t(d_i)$ stand for the position of the color in the sorted color table after step t. This is computed by sorting the d values into the sorted list c_i.

What happens at each step? A color is removed from the sorted list. At the first step, $P_0(d_1)$ is calculated and then the sorted version of d_1 is removed from the sorted list of c values. This is repeated multiple times and the results are combined into a unique number:

$$\sum_{i=1}^{n-1} (P_{i-1}(d_i) - 1)(n - i)!$$

Here's a quick example. Let the color table have four colors: $d_1 = (140, 20, 130)$, $d_2 = (100, 130, 50)$, $d_3 = (250, 14, 12)$, and $d_4 = (22,200, 180)$. When these are sorted, $c_1 = d_4, c_2 = d_2, c_3 = d_1$, and $c_4 = d_3$.

The first step is to locate d_1 in the sorted list and then remove it. $P_0(d_1) = 3$. Then, the next step is to locate d_2 in the sorted list minus

d_1, also known as c_3. In this case, $P_1(d_2) = 2$. The removals affect d_3 and $P_2(d_3) = 2$. The value for the last color, d_4, is guaranteed to be 1 and so it is not included in the unique number:

$$(3 - 1) \times 3! + (2 - 1) \times 2! + (2 - 1) \times 1! = 15$$

This numbering scheme is similar to a progressive basis. In a standard representation of a number in base k, each position contains a value between 0 and $k - 1$. The ith position is worth K^i. In this scheme, the least significant position can be a 0 or a 1. The next most significant can be either a 0, 1 or 2. The next after that can be a 0, 1, 2, or 3, etc.

The algorithm for converting a unique number into the permutation is similar. The number should first be changed from its normal base 10 or base 2 representation into a flexible basis. This is accomplished in a similar way to converting between normal bases. Instead of dividing by k^i to determine the ith position and saving the remainder, the algorithm divides by $i!$ and saves the remainder.

Here's a quick example that converts 315 in base 10 into a flexible basis. There will be five "digits" because $5! = 120$ and $6! = 720$. The fifth position is 2 because $5!$ goes into 300 twice, leaving a remainder of 75. The fourth position is 3 because $4!$ goes into 75 three times, leaving a remainder of 3. The third position is 0, the second position is 1, and the first position is also 1. 315 in base 10 becomes 23011 in the progressive basis.

When the value in the progressive basis is known, then it can be converted into the color permutation. Begin with a list of the colors in sorted order. Let b_i be the "digit" in the ith position. Start with the leftmost, or most significant "digit" and work to the right. At each step, take the ith "digit", select that color from the sorted list, place it in the final list, and remove it. Continue until all of the numbers are exhausted.

The example can be continued. If there are six colors, $c_1, \ldots, c_6$, then the value 315 in base 10 can be converted into this color table: $c_3, c_5, c_1, c_4, c_6, c_2$. These were assembled by selecting them from the sorted list according the value from converting 315 into $23,011$ in a progressive basis.

Tweaked Color Tables

This chapter has shown how to hide information in a pixel by fiddling with the least significant bits of the data in the pixel. There is no reason why this can't be applied to the color table itself. If there are 256 colors in a standard table specified with 24 bits of accuracy, then there are 768 least significant bits available in the table for use. Modifying these bits to hide a tag will not change the appearance of the image in a major way. In fact, it may be quite simple to grab two least significant bits for each component and store 1536 bits.

Summary

Color modification is a deep and interesting subject. The human eye shows a great ability to adapt to subtle changes and filter them out of the signal. The eye may be very sensitive to very minor changes in color when the minor changes are placed in front of it for comparision, but it is also highly adaptive to big changes.

This chapter described several basic mechanisms for changing the color at a pixel in order to store information there. The greatest weakness of this chapter is the lack of study of the effects of the changes on the human visual system. Minor changes are simply assumed to be all right because they're so minor. To a large extent, the small change in the least significant bit better not affect the image because it's the smallest change that can be made.

A more thorough investigation of this subject might begin with a better model for how the eyes perceive colors. If this is understood, then it may be possible to do a much better job adding subtle changes to the colors in order to send information.

Chapter 10

Grouping Bits

Chapters 7 and 9 show how to hide one or two bits of information in locations. This chapter shows how to hide more information by grouping these bits together.

There are many opportunities to hide a small amount of information in one place. Chapter 9, for instance, describes how to hide a few bits in a pixel by modifying the least significant bits. There are many other places where only a few bits will fit in each location, but they come with many locations that can be grouped together. Images come with many pixels. Sound files come with many moments. If there are many images in a collection, then each may hide only a few bits of data from the tag. This chapter describes how to group multiple places together to hide more information.

There are two types of schemes described in this chapter. The first type chooses the order of the data. It might specify, for instance, that the first three bits go in pixel $(0, 0)$, the second three bits go in pixel $(0, 14)$, the third three bits in pixel $(1, 21)$, etc. These scrambling arrangements make it virtually impossible to reassemble the tag without understanding the algorithm used to determine the locations.

The second type of scheme groups multiple pixels together to make the hidden information more robust. At the simplest level, this approach applies the error-correcting codes described in Chapter 5. In more complicated solutions, many of the modulation schemes used in frequency base radio can be applied.

The chapter will treat the individual "packets" of data as "pixels" even though there is no reason why the system can't be used in other places. Audio files are another good location for plenty of noise. Text files have a few places. Any other method of hiding information could be used where it is appropriate and the algorithms from this solution can be used to spread out the data into multiple parts.

For the sake of simplicity, these packets of data or pixels will be labeled $p_1, p_2, \ldots, p_n$. Although most images are two-dimensional arrays of pixels, they can be relabeled as a one-dimensional array to make analysis a bit easier. Most of the algorithms are merely structured to spread out the data in an image, so spreading them out in a one-dimensional array is close to spreading them out in a two-dimensional array.

Also, each pixel or packet will be assumed to hold one bit of data to make analysis simpler. Obviously, many pixels may hold more, but this fact is not necessary to developing algorithms for breaking up information across multiple pixels. These bits will be labeled $d_1, d_2, d_3, \ldots, d_m$.

Random Walks

The section beginning on page 137 describes how to choose a subset if $m < n$.

The simplest solution is to start at pixel p_1 and store d_1 in it. Then put d_2 in p_2, d_3 in p_3, etc. For the sake of simplicity, assume that the number of data bits, m, is equal to the number of pixels n. This algorithm works quite well and it may be sufficiently robust to deter most people. If the attackers can't determine whether the least significant bits were modified, then they won't be able to assemble the data.

The greatest danger, however, is that the attackers will remove the data from each pixel and reassemble it in a file. If the data was mixed into the pixels in sequential order, then the attackers will have complete access to it. If it is ASCII data, then they can read it and even modify it to suit themselves.

One defense is to encrypt the data before it is mixed in, and those solutions are covered in Chapter 2. The encryption algorithms are robust solutions that have been studied in great depth. They should be used in all cases where real security is desirable. They also provide a measure of deception. The output of a good encryption function should be indistinguishable from random noise. Encrypted bits should be indistinguishable from the least significant bits of a sufficiently random image.

Scrambling the order in which data is mixed into the pixels is a solution described here. Instead of placing the data in order, the bits can be mixed in according to a pattern determined by a random walk. Bit d_1 might go in p_{143}, bit d_2 might go in p_{14}, bit d_3 might go in p_{1412}, etc.

This is the process of creating a random permutation of the pixels, p_i, and it can be applied in a number of ways. One approach is to use the permutation as a key like a one-time pad. One party can assemble the permutation and then distribute a copy to everyone who needs it. This can be inconvenient if there are going to be many different permutations used in different circumstances and it can also be impractical if multiple people are going to need a copy. But it can be a workable solution if only one party will need a copy. If a company was watermarking its images, for instance, then it could use a proprietary permutation.

Creating a permutation of the color table is described on page 132.

Here is a simple algorithm for creating a random permutation of pixels. It can be created by building an array of n integers, $a[i]$, such that $a[i] = i$ at the beginning. Two random numbers, x and y, both less than n are chosen. A pseudorandom number generator like those summarized in Knuth's source book [Knu81] is a good beginning. More security-conscious people can either use a physical source of noise and/or encrypt the random bit stream to add more "randomness".

After the two numbers are chosen, the values of $a[x]$ and $a[y]$ are swapped. Then two new random numbers are selected. This is repeated until the permutation is sufficiently "random." Knowing when to stop is beyond the scope of this book and it is the topic of a certain amount of philosophical debate about the nature of randomness. One rule of thumb is to choose at least $4n$ pairs of random numbers so each number is swapped about eight times on average.

Spreading Random Walks

In many cases, the amount of data to be hidden will be less than the number of places it can be stored and the information can be spread out. The simplest way to use the extra space is to spread out the data over the available pixels and use only the pixels that are necessary. This spreads out the disruption of the pixels that may be caused by storing data in them.

The simplest solution is to skip pixels in order. Here's an algorithm. Let $c = \frac{(n-m)}{m}$ be the number of pixels to be skipped for every pixel that gets data. If there are 200 pixels ($n = 200$) and 50 bits of data ($m = 50$), then three pixels will be skipped for each pixel that gets data. If $n = 60$ and $m = 50$, then $c = .2$. Let C be the accumulator that maintains a count of how many pixels to be skipped.

For each pixel, do the following. If C is greater than or equal to 1, then skip a pixel and subtract 1 from C. Otherwise store data in the pixel and add c to C.

This algorithm will spread out the data over available pixels in a uniform fashion. This will be a problem only if the process of storing data in a pixel is detectable. For instance, if the image consists of a solid color, then even a small change in the least significant bit may be apparent to the eye. The regularity of the changes produced by this algorithm will leave a strong pattern that may amplify the changes and make them more apparent.

The process can be randomized. A random quantity can be added to C at the same time that c is added. The random quantity modulates the position and assures that the modified pixels won't be located in a predictable pattern. The size of the random quantity determines the spacing between modified pixels. One simple solution fixes the random quantity to be a value between $-0.5c$ and c. This solution is simple and a more robust solution may use more complicated random distributions.

The scrambling algorithm described in the previous section and the spacing algorithm presented here act independently of each other. Either one can be used separately or both can be combined to produce the right effect.

Error Correction

Error-correcting codes are described in detail in Chapter 5 and the codes are often a good tool for hiding information that may be used to tag a copyrighted item. Small errors occur occasionally as data flows around the network and large errors may be introduced by someone trying to destroy the tags in an image. Error-correcting codes can add some redundancy that defends against both of these cases.

A typical error-correcting code would be applied during the tag creating process before the bits, $d_1 \ldots d_m$ are determined. The net effect of this is similar to that of some of the spread spectrum systems developed for analog radio communication. For instance, if the system uses a simple block code that adds three parity bits to four regular bits, then the data is effectively spread across seven locations. If one location is changed, then the other six can fix it.

This approach can work independently of the process of scrambling the bits and spacing them out randomly, but it may work best in concert with it. A simple error-correcting code will produce blocks of k bits that must be decoded simultaneously. If the bits are arranged along a random walk through the pixels, then any local disturbance will not affect an entire block. It may hit one bit only per block.

The RealAudio system for delivering audio messages across the Internet uses a similar approach to reduce the effects of errors. The signal is sliced into multiple pieces, but only a small sliver of each piece is put into each packet. If a packet is lost, the parts from another packet can be used to interpolate.

Hiding Information in Locations

Most of the techniques described in this chapter store some data in a pixel. Another approach is to store data in the choice of the pixel. For instance, imagine this simple algorithm for encoding a tag between 0 and 3 into an image file.

Value	Pixels Changed
0	p_{142}, p_{502}
1	p_{12}, p_{1003}
2	p_{512}, p_{2212}
3	p_{34}, p_{199}

The pixels can be "changed" in any fashion that could be detected later. The simplest solution is to keep some master version of the image and look for the subtle changes. A more complicated solution is to choose 254 colors to represent the image and then use the 255th and 256th colors as changes.

This example is somewhat arbitrary and it is not easy to extend to a larger number of tags. A more robust system would include some function that would control the relationship between the pixels to be changed and the numbers. Here's a list of possible functions:

Linear Maps To store value i, flip pixel p_i.

More Robust Linear Maps To store value i, flip pixels p_{2i} and p_{n-2i-1} where n is the number of pixels in the image. This solution can store only values between 1 and $\frac{n}{2}$.

Wraparound Maps To store value i, flip pixel $p_{ki \bmod n}$ where k and n have no common divisors other than 1.

Resistance to Detection

One major advantage to this approach is that it resists tampering with the tags. Consider the more robust linear functions that flip one pixel, p_i, to store the value i. If attackers recover two different copies of the image, they may try to erase the tags from both images to get an untagged image. In some cases, it will be impossible to do this.

Consider, for instance, two images encoded with the tag values i and j. This means that pixels p_i and p_j will be different when the two images are compared. When the attacker tries to synthesize a new image, there is no way to determine the unmarked values of these two pixels. The attacker will be forced to choose one value for each of the pixels from either of the images and there are four possible outcomes. In one of the cases, the attacker will choose the "unmarked" value for both pixels and create a clean, unmarked image. In two cases, the attacker will end up choosing the "marked" value for one of the pixels, and in one case, the attacker will choose both "marked" values. In three of the four cases, the new synthetic image will be just as marked.

The approach can be made more secure if more than one pixel is used to mark each document. The simple approach of flipping, say p_{2i} and p_{n-2i-1}, is not a good solution because there is a fairly obvious mathematical relationship between the positions of the pixels. A better solution is to reduce the relationship between the location of the bits. The first marking pixel may be stored between pixels p_1 and $p_{n/2}$ and the second between $p_{n/2}$ and p_n. One could use a direct linear relationship and the other could use a method that wraps around.

More pixels mean more chances that an attacker will carry over some tags from both images. If there are two marking pixels in an image, then the attacker will find four differences between the pixels in the two images. If the attacker randomly chooses values for these four pixels from either image, then only 1 out of 16 choices will leave an unmarked image. One half of the choices will include at least one marking pixel from both images, effectively identifying the source.

This solution begins to fail when the attacker gains access to more than two images. The attacker can examine three or more images and choose the value for the pixel that is contained in the majority of the images.

Frequency Modulation

Multiple values can be stored in the differences between pixels. For instance, the set of values i, j, and k can be hidden in an image by flipping pixels p_i, p_{i+j}, and p_{i+j+k}. This is somewhat similar in spirit to the process of modulating the frequency of a radio wave by making the frequency go faster and slower to encode information.

This can be extended to handle any number of pixels at the cost of the size of the values being stored. In this case, the maximum values of i, j, and k must add up to less than n. This tradeoff is generally worth taking because the number of possible variations that is stored is $i \times j \times k$, which is often much larger than n.

Modified Dithering

Many graphics algorithms use *dithering* to take an image created with a higher amount of precision and reduce it to one that uses a lower amount. Many newspapers, for instance, use half-toning algorithms to convert gray-scale photographs into collections of dots that are precisely arranged to provide the same effect. More dots are concentrated in the darker parts of the image and less in the lighter parts. This allows a printing press to produce an image that seems to have many gray levels while using only one saturated black ink.

Dithering and many other important details from computer graphics are described in [FvDFH82, Gla90, Arv91].

The dithering process is relatively straightforward and it also provides plenty of opportunity to store information. The basic dithering algorithm uses a matrix of points and turns a subset of them on or off to best approximate the intensity at that location. Figure 10.1 shows the possible states for a 2×2 matrix.

There are five possible intensities that can be represented by a 2×2 matrix: 0, $\frac{1}{4}$, $\frac{1}{2}$, $\frac{3}{4}$, and 1. When a gray-scale image is dithered using this black and white matrix, each pixel is replaced by a 2×2 grid of points with the closest approximation to the intensity. So a pixel with a gray-

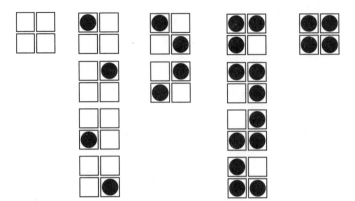

Figure 10.1. The possible states for a 2 × 2 dithering matrix. There are five possible intensities (0, 0.25, 0.5, 0.75, 1.0). Some of the matrices have several possible ways to represent the same intensity and these choices can be used to encode information.

scale value of 56 in a pixel with eight bits that ranges between 0 and 255 would be replaced with a matrix with one dot effectively encoding a level of $\frac{1}{4}$.

The process of converting 56 into $\frac{1}{4}$ effectively rounds off the pixel. $\frac{1}{4}$ is much closer to 64. This error is small, but it can hurt the quality of the image. A large part of the sky may have an intensity value of, say, 33. The algorithm must choose between replacing it with a 2 × 2 matrix approximation of either 0 or $\frac{1}{4}$. Neither is particularly close.

One solution is called *Floyd-Steinberg error diffusion* [FS75]. The error in each pixel is split up between neighboring pixels that haven't been dithered yet. For instance, imagine that the dithering process begins at the upper lefthand corner of an image and proceeds left to right across the rows, attacking the rows in turn from top to bottom. When the algorithm reaches a pixel, all of the pixels above it and to its left have already been replaced by matrices.

The Floyd-Steinberg algorithm takes the error left over from diffusing the data and spreads it out between the neighboring pixels. Figure 10.2 shows the process of splitting up the error. $\frac{7}{16}$ is placed in the pixel in the same row to the right. The three pixels in the next row below get $\frac{3}{16}$, $\frac{5}{16}$, and $\frac{1}{16}$, respectively. Spreading out the information to unprocessed pixels saves the trouble of reprocessing the old pixels. Choosing the best approximation could be done with a least-

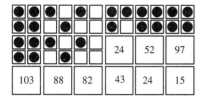
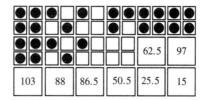

Figure 10.2. Here is a segment of a bitmap before and after the pixel with intensity 24 is dithered. In this case, it is replaced with a matrix with effective value 0 so the 24 units of gray are distributed as an error to the neighbors.

squared, relaxation algorithm but that is much more computationally complicated. This solution is simpler.

Hiding Tagging Data

Most versions of dithering use only one possible matrix for each intensity level. There is a great deal of effort put into choosing the best possible matrix to avoid strange visual effects produced as the dots inadvertently line up. But, as Figure 10.1 demonstrates, there is more than one possible choice for matrices to represent each intensity level. Tagging information can be hidden in this choice.

For instance, there are four possible choices for a matrix with one dot in it and also four possible choices for a matrix with three dots in it. Tagging data can be encoded into the half-tone image by choosing between the four possible choices. Two bits can be stored for every 2×2 matrix that is used in these cases.

There is only one possible matrix for values with intensities of 0 and 1. The 2×2 matrix can either be filled or left empty. But no information can be encoded in this case. Any tagging algorithm could simply skip over these pixels.

A pixel with an intensity of close to $\frac{1}{2}$ can be approximated by filling half of the blocks in a 2×2 matrix with dots. Figure 10.1 shows just two balanced possibilities. There are also four others that are not shown. These two balanced matrices could be used to encode one bit of tagging data every time a choice is made.

What about the other four "unbalanced" matrices? These could be used instead of the other two matrices to encode two bits of tagging information. Can all six be used and store even more bits? Yes. Figure

The process of making choices using a tree is also used in Chapter 8 to choose between words in a grammar-based system.

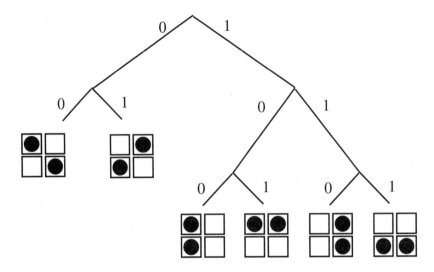

Figure 10.3. Here is a tree that maps the six possible 2 × 2 matrices with two dots into possible bit strings. The method is inspired by Huffman coding.

The tree in Figure 10.3 was inspired by Huffman coding which is described beginning on page 44.

10.3 shows the six possible dot arrangements placed in a tree. The relationship between the bits that are encoded and the arrangement of dots in the matrix is defined by the path from the top of the tree to the bottom. The two bits, "01", for instance, refer to the 2 × 2 matrix with two dots along the diagonal running between the lower left and the upper right corners. The three bits, "101", refer to the matrix with the two dots along the top.

This scheme encodes 2.5 bits on average whenever a pixel is approximated with a dithering matrix of $\frac{1}{2}$. The one of the two "balanced" matrices will appear about 50% of the time and the one of the four "unbalanced" matrices will appear the other 50% of the time. This equal weighting is desirable because an uneven distribution can add visual effects and skew an image.

This chapter has examined only 2 × 2 matrices. Larger matrices mean better approximations and they should be used when possible. The approach can be extended to larger matrices with little trouble, but there may be some aesthetic consequences. Video screens can handle half-toning algorithms with little problem because they're able to place dots in any position with little problems. Printing presses and laser printers, however, may not react well to some dot patterns. Ink and toner can bind together and fill in narrow gaps. The industry developed many solutions to this approach that are beyond the scope of this book. Tuning the approaches presented here to the individual printing methods is left to the readers. It may not be an easy process.

Patchwork

One of the most interesting algorithms comes from Walter Bender, Daniel Gruhl, Norishige Morimoto, and Anthony Lu. Their approach, which they call Patchwork, attempts to skew the statistical profile of an image without disturbing much of the image itself. Their modifications are presumably too small to be noticed by the eye, but large enough to distort the statistical profile.

They begin with the assumption that this value should approach zero:

$$S = \sum_{i=1}^{n} a_i - b_i$$

where a_i and b_i are the intensities at randomly chosen points from the image. As more points are chosen and added to the sum, the result should approach zero if the data in the image is randomly distributed. They make some stiff assumptions about images. They assume that all intensities are equally likely and all samples are "independent of all other samples."

They propose repeatedly choosing points at random and moving one unit of intensity from one to the other. That is, repeatedly choosing point x and point y and adding one unit of intensity to point x while subtracting one unit from y. If this is done repeatedly, the value of S will approach $2n$, a value that is significantly different from 0, the expected value when the image was filled with all intensities.

The main advantage of this approach is immunity to cropping. If the shifting is done throughout the image on a random basis, then the same statistical shift in S should occur in all subsets. The approach begins to fail rapidly, however, if an image is translated, rotated, or projected because these algorithms involve averaging pixels to anti-alias them. This destroys the effect.

Summary

There may be almost as many schemes for grouping the hidden information in n pixels together as there are permutations of n items. This chapter concentrated on some of the major solutions, but it did not investigate each of them in the detail necessary. To some extent, these details are left up to the implementer in much the same way that the composer leaves room for the musician to interpret the piece.

The summary to Chapter 11 compares the advantages and disadvantages of wave-based encoding to the process of randomly selecting pixels out of the image.

Chapter 11

Wave Techniques

This chapter explores how to model a sound file or an image file with a set of wave-like functions. These can often be manipulated to store data in a way that is much more resistant to attack.

Catch a Wave

Here is a snippet from the commentary provided by John Mesh and Rollie Dharma at the World Surfing Competition. John Mesh became famous as the announcer leading the nightly soft news show, "Entertainment, Entertainment", and producing a best-selling recording of show tunes. His career in sports commentary began at the 1996 summer Olympics, where he stole the show as the announcer of the women's gymnastics competition. Rollie Dharma, on the other hand, won four worldwide surfing competitions before retiring after hitting his head on a rock at the bottom of the ocean when he wiped out on a wave that was much too radical.

JM: It's clear that the ocean's rage is bearing down heavily upon the shore this afternoon. Poseidon is really trying to send a message with the waves that pound upon the land with an unceasing rhythm. Humans treat the ocean as their dumping ground for toxic waste or garbage and Poseidon may be sending a cry for help with these 18-foot waves.

RD: The surf is really gnarly.

JM: Yes, it's a message for humanity to stop strip-mining the oceans of the fish and return the control of the ocean's destiny to the oceans themselves. If I read the surf correctly, I see a call for us to stop fencing in the waters of the sea with our mechanical monsters and come to a harmonic convergence with waters.

RD: I see a really nasty left break. That's going to keep our boys on their toes.

JM: Yes, the lord of the deep is sending a challenge to our surfers, a not-so-gentle reminder that we must respect the motion of the waves because they come from a hidden spot in the center of the ocean wherein man does not dwell. This secret spot is Poseidon's lair, where the whales and the dolphins frolic.

RD: I got nudged by a dolphin once.

JM: I wonder what message the dolphin was sending. Whoa. This is the biggest wave I've seen today. It's huge.

RD: Absolutely incredible.

JM: I don't think we should have placed our broadcast booth so close to the ocean.

RD: It keeps building in size.

JM: I wonder what message the ocean is sending now. Uh. We better run.

Wave-Based Tagging

Chapter 9 describes how to hide information in an image's pixel by flipping its least significant bit and Chapter 10 describes how to mix several pixels together to send a more complicated message. Another popular method of encoding information in an image or an audio file is to add a subtle wave carrying information to the signal. The technique is analogous to sending a message over the radio by adding a wave to the radio carrier signal. In this case, the data becomes the carrier instead of some part of the electromagnetic spectrum.

This approach is quite popular with electrical engineers, who have a well-developed set of equations at their disposal. Many electrical engineering concepts are explained through wave functions and it is natural to extend their use into sound and images. The notion of hiding information in the process is also a natural application because radio engineers have spent years understanding *spread spectrum* broadcasting solutions. These ideas were originally pioneered by the military because they helped strengthen a signal against jamming as well as made the signal harder to intercept. Today, spread spectrum solutions are becoming common in consumer electronics like portable phones and the next generation of digital cell phones.

The term *spread spectrum* encompasses a wide variety of techniques and it would be impossible to do the topic justice in this book. A good introduction is the *Spread Spectrum Communications Handbook* by Marvin Simon, Jim Omura, Robert Scholtz, and Barry Levitt [SOSL94]. One popular solution is *frequency hopping*, which hides a signal by rapidly switching the frequency carrying the signal. Both the receiver and the sender need to synchronize their jumps between frequencies to keep the data flowing. The rapid hopping ensures that there will be little competition between one pair of people in communication and another pair because they will rarely be on the same frequency.

This solution is imitated by the technique for hiding information in a subset of the pixels described in Chapter 10. Tagging data can be hidden by jumping from pixel to pixel according to some random walk determined by a shared formula. Multiple messages can be packed together if different random walks are chosen. The odds of interaction are low and the few interactions that mess up the message can be fixed with error-correcting codes.

Another important spread spectrum solution is often called *direct sequence* spread spectrum. This imagines the existence of some carrier wave and the distorts the carrier wave by two other functions, $f(x)$ and $g(x)$. For simplicity, imagine the carrier wave to be $\sin(x)$. Let $f(x)$ be a square wave driven by a pseudo-random number bitstream. Call these bits $f_1, f_2, \ldots$. Let $f(x)$ be 1 for $\alpha i \leq x < \alpha(i+1)$ if f_i is 1 and let $f(x)$ be -1 if f_i is 0. The purpose of $f(x)$ is to add some random noise that makes it impossible for an attacker to intercept the signal. Figure 11.1 shows a simple example of direct sequence spread spectrum. Both sides of the channel must share the same bitstream and have a method for synchronizing the streams.

The function $g(x)$ is the message composed from the bitstream $g_1, g_2, \ldots$. Let $g(x)$ be 1 for $\beta i \leq x < \beta(i+1)$ if g_i is 1 and let $g(x)$ be -1 if g_i is 0. In this case, α and β are different values that must be set large enough to make detection possible. Their size depends, to a large extent, on the quality of the channel.

The greatest interest in spread spectrum techniques exists because the information is spread out across a number of pixels in the image. The process of adding a wave-like signal to the image affects a number

Joshua Smith and Barrett Comiskey describe a technique they call predistortion by which the carrier wave is compressed and uncompressed with JPEG. This reduces the distortive effects of JPEG on images containing direct sequence images.

Many other systems in this book can also use a pseudo-random bitstream to mix up the signal.

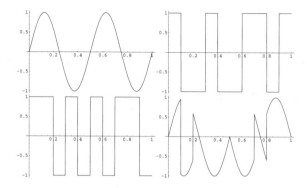

Figure 11.1. The four graphs here show the four parts to a direct-sequence spread spectrum. The upper left is the carrier, $\sin(4\pi x)$. The upper right is $f(x)$, the pseudo-random scrambling function. The lower right is $g(x)$, the data. The lower right shows $f(x)g(x)\sin(4\pi x)$, which is added to the signal.

of pixels and this makes the result more resistant to any interference. The wave signal may still be quite detectable even if a number of the pixels are modified through either signal error or the effects of some malicious tag destroyer.

Here's a simple abstract illustration. Figure 11.2 shows the result of adding together two simple sine waves: $\sin(x) + 0.1\sin(10x)$. The simple sine wave, $\sin(x)$, is often called the *carrier*. The faster wave, $\sin(10x)$, carries the signal. In this case, the signal is the value 0.1.

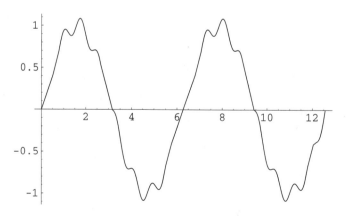

Figure 11.2. The function $\sin(x) + 0.1\sin(10x)$. The basic sine wave acts as the carrier and the faster sine wave acts as the signal.

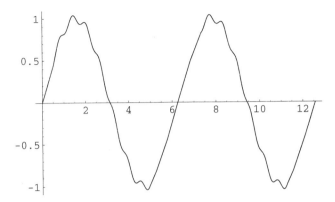

Figure 11.3. The function $\sin(x) + 0.05\sin(10x)$. There is not much difference between this and Figure 11.2.

Figure 11.3 shows a similar version, $\sin(x) + 0.05\sin(10x)$. The multiple of $\sin(10x)$ is now smaller and it has less effect on the main wave. Now, the "signal" could said to be 0.05. This shows a simple way that a number can be shipped in a carrier. In either case, the major carrier, $\sin(x)$, is not disturbed too much. Many of the approaches in this chapter are not much different from this, in an abstract sense. The value, either 0.1 or 0.05, is the tag.

There are many more sophisticated approaches to encoding data over the length of a signal. For instance, the strength of this main signal can change over time to encode information. This is often called *amplitude modulation* and it is also the basis for sending music or talk and voice over AM radios. Figure 11.4 shows a function $\sin(8x)(1 + .5\sin(2x))$. The function $\sin(8x)$ is considered the *carrier* and the function $(1 + .5\sin(2x))$ would be considered the *signal*. Or, in the parlance of this book, the tag.

In the simple example of Figure 11.4, the signal does not change over time. In reality, it would change often. The amplitude of the carrier would grow when the music boomed and it would shrink when people spoke softly.

The figure also illustrates a basic problem in many electronic arenas: aliasing. The carrier wave oscillates only four times faster than the signal wave. This means that the amplitude of the signal can be sampled only at four locations during the length of the signal. In the figure, these moments can be seen when the carrier wave ($\sin(8x)$) touches the outside envelope ($\pm(1 + .5\sin(8x))$ drawn only for illustration purposes.

AM radios do not mix together two signals. They just change the amplitude of the carrier.

The figures in this chapter are generated using Mathematica, a very nice program for mathematics research from Wolfram Research. See www.mathematica-.com *for ordering information.*

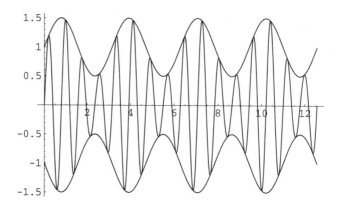

Figure 11.4. The function $\sin(8x)(1 + .5\sin(2x))$ is the function plotted in the middle. The function $\pm(1 + .5\sin(2x))$ forms an envelope and is plotted for illustration purposes.

In real examples, the difference is much more significant. AM radio broadcasts around 1000 kilohertz and carries an audio signal with most of its significant content between .2 and 20 kilohertz. Humans can't generally hear outside this range. This is a factor of about 500, a significantly more accurate solution.

Another common signaling system is known as *frequency modulation*, a process which changes the frequency of the carrier wave. Figure 11.5 shows the function $\sin(4x + .5\sin(2x))$ plotted as a thick gray line. The normal, unmodulated position of the carrier is shown as a thin, black line. The warbling of the thick black line carries the information.

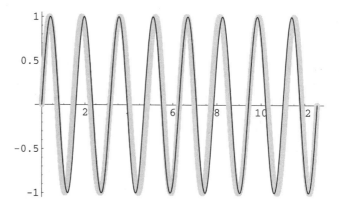

Figure 11.5. The function $\sin(4x + .5\sin(x))$ is plotted in thick gray and the carrier's normal position $(\sin(4x))$ is plotted as black.

Fourier Series

The system of adding a small signal can be used to add tagging bits to audio files. If two-dimensional equivalents are used, then it can be used to place tagging bits in an image file. The presence, absence, or strength of the secondary sine function can be easily established by using a well-understood branch of mathematics known as *Fourier analysis*. The basic version shocked the world when it was shown that any smooth function defined between $0 \leq x \leq 2v$ could be represented as the sum of an infinite number of sine or cosine waves with a form like this:

$$f(x) = \frac{c_0}{2} + \sum_{j=-\infty}^{\infty} c_j \sin\left(\frac{j\pi x}{v}\right) + d_j \cos\left(\frac{j\pi x}{v}\right)$$

The only problem is finding the values of c_j and d_j. Today, the field is filled with many fast and accurate algorithms for computing these coefficients given samples of the function at discrete locations. Specialized central processing units known as digital signal processors (DSPs) are optimized to perform this calculation.

The entire field, however, was developed with continuous mathematics and expressed in terms of integral calculus. Here are simple equations for c_j and d_j that may offer many readers some understanding. Calculus is still more common than some forms of discrete analysis. Here are the equations:

$$c_j = \frac{1}{v} \int_0^{2v} f(x) \cos\left(\frac{j\pi x}{v}\right) dx \quad d_j = \frac{1}{v} \int_0^{2v} f(x) \sin\left(\frac{j\pi x}{v}\right) dx$$

Here's a simple example of how the calculation will discover the components. To some extent, the example will seem trivial because the function to be emulated by the Fourier series, $f(x)$, will also be defined in terms of sine waves. The next example will be different.

Figure 11.6 shows a graph of a function $f(x) = \sin(x) + .3\sin(4x)$ on the left. The goal of Fourier analysis is to find the coefficients of c_j and d_j so that the sum of the infinite series will equal $f(x)$ over the range of $0 \leq x \leq 2\pi$. It should come as no surprise that $c_j = 0$ for all j and $d_j = 0$ for most j except $d_1 = 1$ and $d_3 = .3$.

The right side of Figure 11.6 reveals how these values are calculated. These graphs show $f(x)\sin(x)$, $f(x)\sin(2x)$, $f(x)\sin(3x)$, and

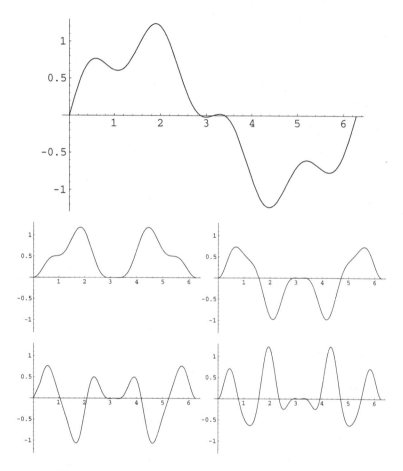

Figure 11.6. Here are a graph of the function $f(x) = \sin(x) + .3\sin(4x)$ above and four graphs of $f(x)$ multiplied by $\sin(x)$, $\sin(2x)$, $\sin(3x)$, and $\sin(4x)$ on the bottom. If the four graphs on the bottom are integrated, the result returns the Fourier coefficients.

$f(x)\sin(4x)$. If these are integrated, they return the amounts $\pi, 0, 0, .3\pi$. You can think of the process as finding out how much of $f(x)$ is represented by the four different sine waves. The first one represents a significant amount, which is why its integral is so large. The second and third come to zero because the parts that are represented are balanced by the parts that are out of alignment. You can think of the part of these graphs above the x-axis as the places where the function $f(x)$ is in sync with the sine wave and the parts where it is below the x-axis as the places where it is out of sync.

There is one point that deserves mentioning. This system works well because the various types of sines and cosines are *orthogonal*. The waves do not interact. This is expressed mathematically as:

$$\int \sin(nx)\sin(mx) = 0 \quad \int \cos(nx)\cos(mx) = 0$$

when $n \neq m$. Also

$$\int \sin(nx)\cos(mx) = 0$$

for all m and n. That means that when the parts of the function are distributed between the different components, there will be only one unique solution.[1]

Discrete Fourier Analysis

Most computer programs do not analyze data on a symbolic level. Although the Fourier series was presented here as a symbolic system of integrals, the practical implementations are structurally very different. They still decompose a function into harmonic components, but they operate on discrete representations. The functions aren't smooth symbolic representations, they're vectors or arrays of data. The result isn't an infinite series, it's just finite.

The standard solution is to use a finite approximation that takes in a finite amount of data (a_j) and returns a finite number of coefficients (b_j). In Mathematica,

$$b_s = \frac{1}{\sqrt{n}} \sum_{r=1}^{n} a_r e^{2\pi i(r-1)(s-1)/n}$$

This representation can be very easy to use because it makes it simple to discover the periodic components of a signal. This combines the sine and cosine functions because $e^{ix} = \cos(\pi x) + i\sin(\pi x)$.

Here's an example from the Mathematica book [Wol96]. The command `Table[N[Sin[30 2 Pi n/256] + (Random[] -.5)],n,256]` creates a table of 256 values from sampling a sine function 256 times during a standard interval between 0 and 2π. This particular sine

I reread Pale Fire *more carefully. I liked it better when expecting less. And what was that? What was that dim distant music, those vestiges of color in the air? Here and there I discovered in it and especially, especially in the invaluable variants, echoes and spangles of my mind, a long ripplewake of my glory. – Vladimir Nabokov,* Pale Fire.

---

[1]The existence of a *unique* solution is an interesting vestigial bit of mathematics. When computers can create exact representations it is a better question to ask whether there is an efficient algorithm for coming up with any solution. Sometimes these algorithms use the notion of uniqueness to solve the problem, but it is not necessarily connected.

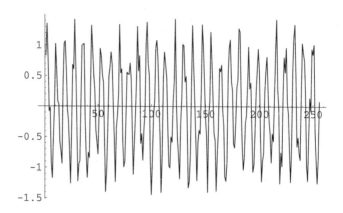

Figure 11.7. A graph of 256 discrete points sampled from the function sin(30x) after being distorted by some random noise.

function oscillates 30 times over the interval. The function itself is mixed up by a fair amount of random noise. Random[] generates a value between 0 and 1. Figure 11.7 shows a plot of a function with a period of 30 units.

The Fourier transform converts the 256 points along the discrete sampling of the function, a_j, into 256 values, b_j, that represent the harmonic structure of the data. The summation replaces the integral.

The values of a are often called the function domain while the values of b are often called the frequency domain because they represent the various frequencies.

Figure 11.8 shows the coefficients calculated by doing the discrete Fourier transform of the noisy version of sin(30x) shown in Figure 11.7. The coefficients are complex numbers and the left side shows the real part of the components and the right side shows the imaginary part.

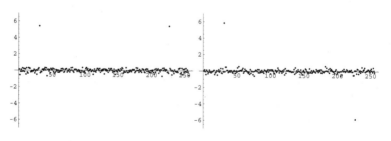

Figure 11.8. The left shows the real part of the coefficients and the right side shows the imaginary part of the coefficients calculated in the Fourier transform of the function shown in Figure 11.7. Notice that most are very small, but there are peaks at the correct frequencies.

There are two large coefficients at 31 and 226. The large coefficient at 31 corresponds to the overall periodic wave of 30 units. (The first coefficient, b_0, is a constant.) The period of $e^{2\pi i 30}$ has a high correlation with the pattern of the function in Figure 11.7 just like the graph of $f(x)\sin(x)$ in Figure 11.6. The large coefficient at 226 represents a kind of reflection caused by the fact that the Fourier algorithm is discrete. This occurs because the equation for b_j has $(r-1)(s-1)$ in the term.

The Fourier transform can be inverted and the combination of the two algorithms is used in many algorithms in audio processing. One of the simplest algorithms is used to filter out unwanted frequencies, by computing the Fourier transform, zeroing out the terms representing the unwanted frequencies, and then using the inverse transform to return to a filtered version of the function.

Fourier transforms are often used for compression. In this case, the signal from Figure 11.9 could be compressed into four numbers.

This next example will do the reverse of this and it will show how a tagging frequency can be manipulated. Figure 11.9 shows a slightly noisy version of $\sin(x) + .1\sin(8x)$ produced by the Mathematica command `Table[N[Sin[ 2 Pi n/256] + .1 Sin[ 8 2 Pi n/256]+.05(Random[] -.5)],n,256]`. This function is sampled 256 times along the range between 0 and 2π.

The real and imaginary parts of the coefficients calculated from the Fourier transform are shown in Figure 11.10. There are four large coefficients, b_2, b_9, b_{249}, and b_{256}. $b_2 = 0.200823 + 8.00264i$, $b_9 = 0.163444 + 0.791083i$, $b_{249} = 0.163444 - 0.791083i$, and $b_{256} = 0.200823 - 8.00264i$. The rest are close to zero.

This example will achieve two goals with one move. The function will be cleaned of noise and the secondary sine wave will be amplified

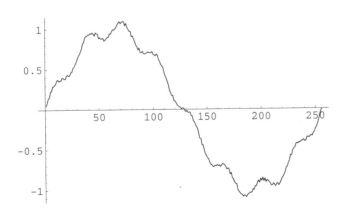

Figure 11.9. A slightly noisy version of $\sin(x) + .1\sin(8x)$.

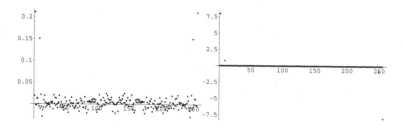

Figure 11.10. The real and imaginary coefficients of the slightly noise function shown in Figure 11.9. Note that there are four peaks in each graph representing the two dominant frequencies.

a bit as a means of injecting a bit of tagging information. This process is used in a more rigorous way with images later in the chapter. To achieve this, the small values of b_j will be zeroed out while the values of b_9 and b_{249} will be doubled.

Figure 11.11 shows the result of taking the inverse Fourier transform of these coefficients after they've been changed. The result is much smoother than Figure 11.9 and the minor wave component of $\sin(8x)$ has been amplified. The process of changing some of the prominent coefficients is one technique for encoding information using the transform. Although this changes the data, it changes only the most significant parts of the data.

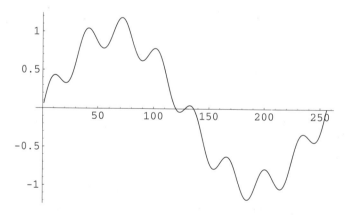

Figure 11.11. The result of computing the inverse Fourier transform of the coefficients in Figure 11.10 after the small coefficients have been zeroed out and the coefficients representing the function $\sin(8x)$ are doubled. This should be similar to Figure 11.9.

One simple analogy is encoding some information in a picture of a face. One solution is to stick a bump or two on a cheek. Another is to lengthen or shorten the nose. The later solution is much less apparent to the viewer.

Two-Dimensional Fourier Transforms

The Fourier transforms in one dimension can be used to hide information in audio files. There is a two-dimensional version that is used extensively in image processing. It can also be used to remove noise or to add signals that may include tagging information. The two-dimensional version of the Fourier transform is similar. The data arrives in a discrete array with terms $a_{p,r}$, where both p and r lie between 1 and n. The array must be square. The equation looks like this:

$$b_{s,t} = \frac{1}{\sqrt{n}} \sum_{p=1}^{n} \sum_{r=1}^{n} a_{p,r} (e^{2\pi i(p-1)(s-1)/n} + e^{2\pi i(r-1)(t-1)/n}).$$

Figure 11.12 shows one of the many two-dimensional wave functions used to assemble a frequency analysis of a two-dimensional function using the Fourier analysis. In this case, it is the real part of $e^{2ix} + e^{3iy}$. There are many combinations of the two.

All of the same techniques for frequency and amplitude modulation can also be applied to images using either one- or two-dimensional Fourier analysis. Each row in the image can be thought of as a one-dimensional signal or the entire image can be thought of as a two-dimensional one. More information can be packed into a one-dimensional approach, but the two-dimensional approach is more robust. It can still convey the tagging bits in the face of cropping or more diverse error.

Wavelets

The Fourier series dominated much of applied mathematics before computers became popular because sines and cosines were easy functions to use. They could be integrated with little trouble. In recent years, however, many mathematicians and computer scientists recognized that there was little reason to limit themselves to simple,

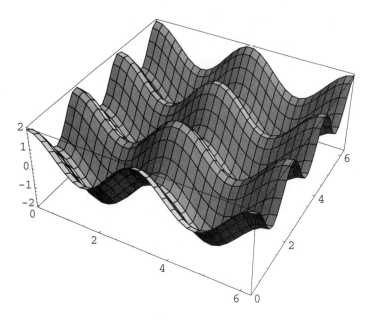

Figure 11.12. One of the many two-dimensional wave functions used to create the two-dimensional Fourier transform. This plot shows the real part of the function $e^{2ix} + e^{3iy}$.

repeating functions. Computers could calculate arbitrary functions to arbitrary levels of precision so it would be possible to decompose some signal or data into another set of functions. Some set may be particularly better than others.

This branch of mathematics has taken the term *wavelet* to mean an arbitrary function that is used to model a bigger function. Many of these wavelets are also orthogonal like the sines and cosines, but some do not. Many of the wavelet decompositions use the same basic function repeated at different scales like the sines and the cosines, but some do not.

One of the biggest differences, however, is the way that wavelets are shrunk. The Fourier series use functions like $\sin(x)$, $\sin(2x)$, ... and when the sine function is shrunk, the wave is just repeated again. The problem is that many functions are not particularly consistent. While the examples from the earlier part of this chapter were quite periodic despite the injection of some random noise, many real-world examples from audio or video signals are far from periodic. The fact that the sine function is repeated again and again may make the process simpler, but it diminishes the efficiency. When the coefficient for $\sin(2x)$ is computed, it must be a balance of how well the first repetition of the sine function fits the domain between 0 and π and how well the sine function fits the domain between π and 2π. The coefficient is trying to summarize how well the sine function serves two masters.

This process gets increasingly worse as the frequencies grow. The function $\sin(8x)$ must try to match a pattern that may vary in an arbitrary way with a function that oscillates eight times and repeats itself. The system works well only in theory because there is an infinite number of terms to counteract all of the error. In practice, Fourier transforms need many extra terms to represent the data. While nice, periodic functions like the one shown in Figure 11.7 may be easily represented by only a few significant terms, more arbitrary functions like audio signals need too many terms.

Wavelet decompositions avoid some of these problems by shrinking in a flexible way. Instead of forcing one value of a coefficient to control the strength of some part, the parts are split up using what is often called *multi-resolution analysis*. That is, a different coefficient is chosen for $\sin(2x)$ between 0 and π and for it between π and 2π. Four coefficients are chosen for $\sin(4x)$: one for the part of $f(x)$ between 0 and $\frac{\pi}{2}$, one for $\frac{\pi}{2}$ to π, one for π to $\frac{3\pi}{2}$, and one for $\frac{3\pi}{2}$ to 2π.

Figure 11.13 shows three levels of analysis for some hypothetical case where a function, $f(x)$, is modeled with sine waves in the interval between 0 and 2π. Notice that the top row shows the function $\sin(4x)$ being multiplied by four different coefficients for the four different quarter regions.

Figure 11.14 shows the sum of the three different waves in Figure 11.13. Notice how non-periodic the function is over the span of the region.

The graphs in this section were produced using the Wavelet Explorer package for Mathematica written by Yu He.

Other Wavelets

Sine and cosine are far from the only shapes that can be used to take apart functions. Much of the research in wavelets over the last decade focused on defining new shapes and finding how well they can describe certain functions.

One of the most basic shapes is the Haar wavelet. For $0 \leq x < .5$, the wavelet is set to 1. Between $.5 \leq x < 1$, it is set to -1. Figure 11.15

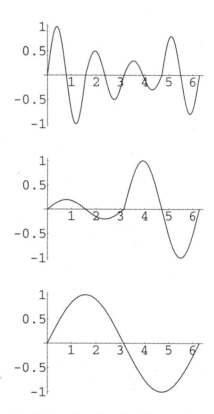

Figure 11.13. A graph of three levels of multi-resolution decomposition of some function. The bottom row shows sin(x). The second row shows sin($2x$) with two different coefficients governing the size of the two halves. The top row shows sin($4x$) multiplied by four different coefficients.

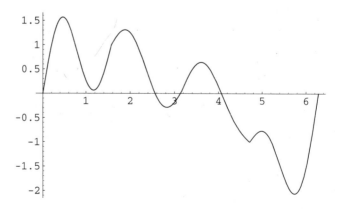

Figure 11.14. The sum of the three different curves shown in Figure 11.13.

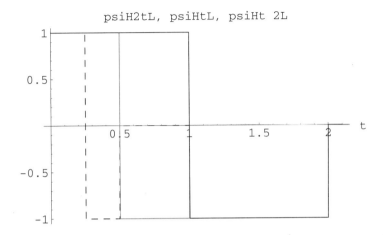

Figure 11.15. Three versions of the Haar wavelet shown with a dashed line ($\psi(2t)$), gray line ($\psi(t)$), or solid line ($\psi(\frac{t}{2})$).

shows the Haar wavelet at three different resolutions. The process of shrinking or growing it is known as *dilation*.

The Haar wavelet has what is called *compact support* and this means that it is non-zero for only a small, bounded amount of the real line. The different versions of the function produced by integer dilation are also *orthogonal*. The three functions shown in Figure 11.15 satisfy the same definition of orthogonality as sines or cosines that are dilated by an integer amount. That is, $\int \psi(jt)\psi(kt)dt = 0$ for j not equal to k.

The Haar wavelet is not particularly interesting because it is just a flat line. It is not as much a system for representing functions as it is just a different way of looking at them. If there are, for instance, 256 samples of a function in a region, then there are eight different resolutions for Haar wavelets to model the function. At resolution j, the function is sampled every 2^j samples. If $j = 0$, then we have all 256 samples. If $j = 2$, then there are 64 samples produced by keeping every fourth sample.

Other wavelets can produce better results. Figure 11.16 shows a Meyer wavelet constructed with a small approximation. The approximate formula is: .33 (-0.383 Cos[2.62 (-0.5+t)]-0.924 Cos[3.67 (-0.5+t)]-0.981 Cos[4.71 (-0.5+t)]-0.831 Cos[5.76 (-0.5+t)]-0.556 Cos[6.81 (-0.5+t)]-0.195 Cos[7.86 (-0.5+t)]). The approximate formula was constructed by the Mathematica function using a Fourier expansion so it looks like a string of cosine functions.

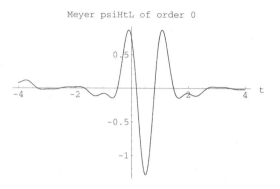

Figure 11.16. The Meyer wavelet

There are also two-dimensional wavelets that are produced by multiplying two functions together. For instance, Figure 11.17 shows a one-dimensional wavelet produced by the Mathematica function `LeastAsymmetricFilter` function and converted into a wavelet. Figure 11.18 shows a two-dimensional version produced by multiplying the function: $\psi(x)\psi(y)$.

Most of the field of wavelets lies outside the scope of this book, which is interested only in presenting the fact that 1) data can be modeled as a sum of a collection of functions and 2) some of the coefficients of these functions can be modified to encode information without radically altering the appearance of the data.

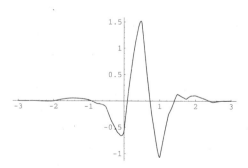

Figure 11.17. A one-dimensional wavelet, $\psi(x)$. A two-dimensional version can be found in Figure 11.18.

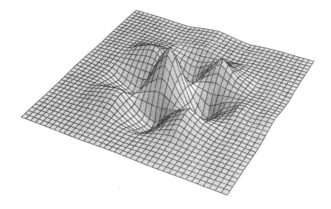

Figure 11.18. A two-dimensional version of the function in Figure 11.17: $\psi(x)\psi(y)$.

Encoding Data

The goal of this book is to explore ways to add tagging information to data in a way that does not destroy the basic appearance of the data to the person using it. The tagging information may be used to carry information about the copyright holder of a particular block of data or it might even carry individualized information about the license holder in order to track illicit copies. Wave-based solutions can be ideal in many cases because the wave functions often do a good job of capturing the structure of the underlying data. Pictures often have large, prominent features and these can often be modeled well with large, prominent waves. Audio signals can also be described fairly well by a set of waves.

This part of the book works with images by thinking of them as a set of coefficients produced by some wave-based representation of the data. It might be produced by a Fourier transform, a simple cosine transform, or a more sophisticated wavelet approach. In any case, the image, audio file, or block of data isn't thought of as a pile of bits, but as a list of coefficients that are approximations of real numbers.

The process of encoding data can be done by changing the coefficients of the wave functions. This is similar to changing the least significant bits of the individual pixels because it makes little sense to change the coefficients by a great deal. A large change in even one coefficient could add distorted waves throughout the image.

Changing the Coefficients' Least Significant Bits

In fact, one simple approach is to simply change the least significant bits of the coefficients. Assessing the fragility of this approach is a bit more difficult to do in this case. If the least significant bits of the image are turned, then the change is local and limited. But one coefficient controls the amount of effect from one wave function and it often controls this effect over a large region. Changing the coefficient can have much wider effects. Each coefficient also controls a different wave function, so each change will have different effects. Nevertheless, minor changes still have minor effects, no matter how diffuse they may be.

Changing the least significant bit is not particularly robust. Slight changes in an image can affect the coefficients. But the fact that each coefficient is related to a block of data means that small changes in the data may not mean many changes in the coefficients. For instance, changing the least significant bits of each pixel or snippet of sound will not produce significant changes in many of the coefficients for the larger wave functions. They will affect the littlest ones. Error-correcting codes are clearly necessary.

A Sound Example

Figure 11.19 shows a plot of the sound intensity produced by the author saying, "Thanks for buying my book." It was encoded in the Sun audio file format with the 8-bit logarithmic mulaw encoding method.

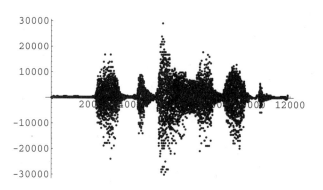

Figure 11.19. A plot of the author saying, "Thanks for buying my book."

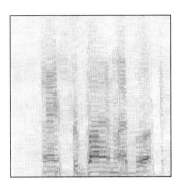

Figure 11.20. The frequencies revealed by the discrete cosine transform applied to the sound data shown in Figure 11.19.
* Actual representation—not an error.

That is, 8 bits can be used to represent intensities with a range of 16 bits. The sound was sampled 8000 times per second for 1.45 seconds, leaving 11,880 samples in the sound file.

The discrete cosine transform for the audio message was calculated using the function CosPacketTransform from the Mathematica Wavelet package. This uses cosine functions and recursively subdivides the audio file until it achieves an adequate representation of the data. Figure 11.20 shows the distribution of the frequencies along the y-axis and the time along the x-axis. The cosine packet transform reveals the different frequencies at each part of the sound file.

Mathematica's Wavelet Explorer package comes with several different wavelet transforms available to use. The sensitivity to errors is easy to test by computing the wavelet transforms before and after some noise is injected. Figure 11.21 shows the percentage change in some of the coefficients after each point in Figure 11.19 is permuted by a random amount of up to 2%. It is clear that the coefficients also change by a small random amount.

This shows that any tagging information added to the coefficients must include a fair amount of error correction and also be fairly significant in size.

Adding Special Frequencies

One popular commercial solution for adding copy protection to either audio or video files is to add a particular pure tone or collection of

Figure 11.21. This graph shows the effects of random noise on the cosine transform of the sound file shown in Figure 11.19. That is, the cosine transform of the original sound file and the cosine transform of the original permuted by some random noise were both calculated. This graph shows the differences, which are small.

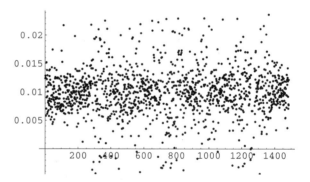

Figure 11.22. This graph is like the graph in Figure 11.21, except it shows the effects upon the wavelet transform using the least asymmetric filter (right).

tones to the file. These tones will be readily apparent in the discrete Fourier transform and it is possible to make decisions based upon their existence.

Figure 11.23 shows the results returned by running the cosine transform algorithm in Mathematica upon the data in Figure 11.19. Two pure tones were injected by changing the coefficients, b_{30} and b_{40}, to $30,000$. Before, the values were around 1000. Then the inverse cosine transform was used to convert it back to an audio file.

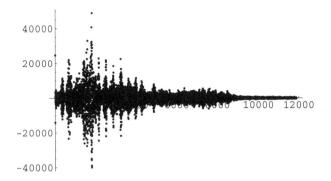

Figure 11.23. The coefficients produced by creating the cosine transform of the data in Figure 11.19.

Figures 11.24 and 11.25 shows a plot of the sound intensities before and after. The left side is equivalent to Figure 11.19, but it is plotted on a shorter range in order to illustrate the effects of injecting the tone. The values in this left plot also fall into discrete levels because they were produced from an 8-bit sound file. [2]

The right plot shows the sound intensities after injecting the two tones. The conversion process has scattered the values outside the 8-bit discrete levels. The two tones can be seen on the left-hand side where there is only silence. The signal is also present in the middle of the talking, but it is not apparent in this image.

Figure 11.24. The plots of the sound intensity before injecting two tones through a cosine transform. The view after is shown in Figure 11.25.

---

[2]They fall in planes, like the rain in Spain. And it doesn't matter what accent you use.

Figure 11.25. The plots of the sound intensity *after* injecting two tones through a cosine transform. The view before is shown in Figure 11.24.

This process adds the tones throughout the file. If the file is cropped or edited, the tones will still be present and detectable by simply taking the discrete cosine transform again. The process also resists a certain amount of noise. To test this, the sound file tagged with two tones had random noise of no more than 5% added to the signal. The discrete cosine transform was computed again. Figure 11.26 shows the smallest coefficients and still shows the peaks at b_{30} and b_{40}.

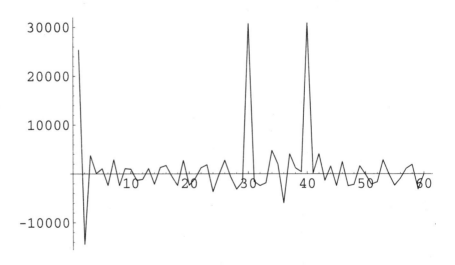

Figure 11.26. The smallest 60 coefficients from the cosine transform *after* adding 5% noise to the sound file tagged by adding two tones. Note the spikes at 30 and 40 units.

More Robust Techniques

The process of simply adding tones may be useful for marking a particular file, but there is not much flexibility. Ideally, the tagging data might include several bytes of data, at a minimum, to identify the owner or provide some more copyright information. There are several approaches to this.

One promising solution was suggested by Ingemar Cox, Joe Kilian, Tom Leighton, and Talal Shamoon [CKLS96]. They worked primarily with the discrete cosine transform of images and modified a number of the most prominent coefficients. The paper suggests that the proper way to tag an image is to use the transforms to identify the most prominent parts of an image and then make the changes there. This seems to be much less detectable than adding noise all over the image.

They add the tagging information by modifying many of the coefficients. In the experiments in their paper, they used a 256×256 pixel image and modified the 1000 largest coefficients produced by a discrete cosine transform. For the sake of simplicity, call these largest coefficients $\{b_i\}$. They modified them with a tagging vector they call a "watermark" that is also 1000 random real numbers, $\{x_i\}$. They offer three equations for computing the new values of the coefficients after tagging, $\{b_i'\}$:

- $b_i' = b_i + \alpha x_i$

- $b_i' = b_i(1 + \alpha x_i)$

- $b_i' = b_i e^{\alpha x_i}$

Each can be inverted as long as $b_i \neq 0$ and so the values can be removed. The second and third equations do a better job of scaling to fit a range of values of b_i. The values of x_i are best kept below 1.

The value of α is a scaling factor that controls how "strong" the tags are. The value of α may be modified in different segments of the image if a windowed transform is computed. Bo Tao and Bradley Dickinson suggest using statistical techniques to identify the regions of the images that are textured (good for adding noise) from those that are filled with sharp edges (bad) [TD96].

Their algorithm calculates a transform of the data, adds in the vector of random watermarks with one of the three equations, and then computes the inverse transform. This will add a small amount of noise throughout the image.

The tagging information is recovered by computing the transform, finding the largest coefficients, and inverting the equation to pull out a vector of values, $\{x'_i\}$. If the image data is unchanged because it was shipped around digitally, then these values of x'_i will be exactly the same.

Many different things can change the image data. Compression with a lossy compression mechanism like JPEG is a major threat on the Net. Printing out the image is another one. There is also a wide variety of rotations and transformation that can modify the data in some way or another. If any of these things happen, the values of x'_i will not be exactly the same as x_i.

But, there will be similarities. They propose a similarity metric for comparing the two vectors:

$$\frac{X' \cdot X}{\sqrt{X' \cdot X'}}$$

where X' symbolizes the vector of x'_i.

How can you tell the difference between one set of tagging information and another? Their process produces a different random vector for each "tag." You can't control the individual bits in the tag. The best matching tag is found by computing the similarity metric to compare the tag in question with each tag in the database.

Their experiments show that even significant degrading does not produce a false result. They tested it by 1) scaling the image, 2) compressing it with JPEG parameters as low as 5% quality and 0% smoothing, 3) dithering the image, and 4) clipping the image. In each case, the one true tag stood out from the other tags in the database.

They also printed out the image, photocopied it, and rescanned it into a computer. The tag was very weak, but it could be amplified by merely looking at the signs of the values of x_i. That is, the values of x_i were converted into a bit vector by mapping the positive values to 1 and the negative ones to -1.

In one of the more interesting experiments, they assumed that some attacker may have access to five copies of the image with different tags. If the attacker averages the five images, then the result still looks quite presentable. But, the tags are still in place and the average image is still closest to the five vectors of tags that produced the image.

Summary

Wave-based methods for taking apart audio and visual data are quite popular and very powerful. They build upon a strong foundation of work developed to send information across the radio spectrum and the techniques in this chapter have not even begun to exploit all of the solutions available. Spread spectrum communications is a big arena and this chapter only touched upon its applications.

There is also a great deal of debate over whether wave-based approaches or pixel-based approaches are better. Obviously, pixel-based approaches that rely upon the least significant bit of each pixel are subject to destruction. An attacker needs only to wipe out the least significant bit of all pixels and the data is gone. But pixel-based solutions are not limited to the least significant bit. They can also introduce deeper changes. All of the changes can use the error-correcting techniques from Chapter 5 to help defend against random destruction.

Wave-based solutions introduce more subtle changes in an image and these changes are also more deeply integrated into the image. The greatest advantage of these solutions is that they can be compressed using the popular JPEG algorithm and still survive. This is an important advantage on the modern, bandwidth-hungry Net.

The disadvantage is that they are much less efficient and carry much less data. Digimarc's system, for instance, stores only 76 real bits in a 256×256 image. If one bit was hidden in each pixel, exactly 8k bytes could be stored away. That's a lot of data and plenty of room for error-correcting codes to defend against random errors.

See page 175 for information about the Digimarc system and how it can be disrupted.

One interesting question is whether a wave-based solution or a random-hopping pixel-based method is better. Clearly, wiping out the least significant bits of every pixel will attack the pixel-based approach. The wave-based approach can still identify the frequency of subtle waves even in the face of random error. These frequencies will still be apparent even in the face of cropping.

But the wave-based approaches are still subject to some greater attacks. The algorithms for modeling the image or sound file with waves are all discrete and are tuned only to finding certain discrete frequencies. They can be fooled if the grid is scaled or rotated in some way. The current algorithms for anti-aliasing can do a good job rotating an image or interpolating detail for a sound file, but this can disrupt the ability of a Fourier transform to identify certain discrete frequencies.

Unfortunately, this area is still in its infancy, so it is hard to make any solid judgments about the relative strengths of each approach. More research is certainly necessary.

Chapter 12

Copyright Software

Many people need an array of professional software. This chapter explores some of the more prominent packages.

This chapter offers a look at some of the software solutions on the market for controlling the copyright. This section is probably incomplete because the industry is rapidly expanding and more and more content providers come to grips with how to control information in a digital wonderland. If your company is not treated in this section, please feel free to contact me so I can include your software in the next edition of the book.

Digimarc

The Digimarc watermarking system is one of the best capitalized projects in the marketplace at this time. The idea was developed by Geoffrey Rhoads, a physicist who worked on many different projects in space imaging. He created the system to watermark his photos so he could track their movement through the Internet. The system is currently built into Adobe's Photoshop 4.0, the most popular image manipulation program on the market.

The system embeds 128 bits of information into each image that is at least 256×256 pixels large. Seventy-six bits are a personalized identification tag and Digimarc maintains a database matching identification tags with names, addresses, and phone numbers. They charge $150 per year at this time to keep a place in the database.

The software is integrated into the Adobe Photoshop software and each image is scanned as it is opened up. If a watermark is found, then a small copyright mark (©) is displayed so that it will be obvious to the user that someone is claiming copyright on the image. The system is automatic, so it is impossible for a user to escape the notice. A separate reader (ReadMarc) is also distributed free from the Digimarc Web site (www.digimarc.com).

Anyone who opens up an image using either Photoshop, Corel, or the ReadMarc package will be able to see if a watermark is present. If there is a watermark, then the copyright status of the image and the identification number of the creator are displayed. If the status is "restricted", then you shouldn't use the image without the creator's permission.

Digimarc's Web page can be used to look up the identification number and discover the name, e-mail address, and telephone number for the official creator of an image.

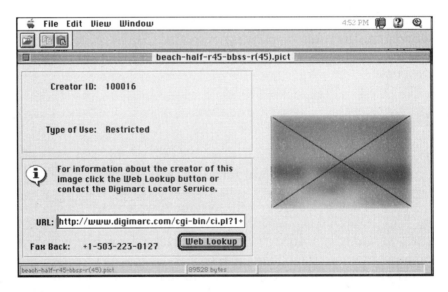

Figure 12.1. This figure shows a screen shot from the Digimarc software after it successfully extracted a watermark id number from an image. The image here is blurred and crossed out because its use is restricted as the software informed the author.

Experimenting with Image Degradation

I tested the Digimarc software by downloading the watermarked image of the day from their Web site and then manipulating it in Adobe Photoshop. The watermark was recovered by the ReadMarc software after these simple situations:

- Saving with an increased amount of compression using the JPEG format.

- Embedding the image in a larger image by surrounding it with whiteness.

- Rotating the image by 45 degrees and then rotating it back.

- Blurring the image twice and then reversing the process by sharpening it twice.

The Digimarc watermark failed to be recovered, however, after I rotated the image, blurred it twice, sharpened it up twice, and then rotated it back to normal. The software detected a watermark, but failed to recover enough information from the ID tag to make an identification. This solution may give someone enough of a hint that someone tagged the image at one time.

This approach did not significantly degrade the quality of the image. A close examination showed that much of the image still appeared to be the same. There were many other cases where even noticeable degradation still left the watermark intact.

If I smeared out the watermark in only half of the image by rotating it and blurring it, the software still recovered the watermark and the correct identification number after both halves were put back together.

The fact that rotation before the blurring removed the watermark is a telling detail. Wave-based tagging algorithms will often use discrete representations of the waves that are aligned along pixel boundaries. Blurring the images after the rotation averages pixels across the normal grid and apparently mixes up the different rows and columns enough to destroy the watermark.

Stego and EzStego

One of the first simple implementations for hiding information with the Macintosh is the Stego program created by Romana Machado, a former software engineer from Apple Computers and something of a Net personality. The program hides information by flipping the least significant bits of an image stored in the classic Macintosh image file format, the PICT. The program uses 24-bit or 8-bit images and calculates the maximum length of data that can be stored away.

The Stego program illustrates some of the problems with using basic least significant bit arithmetic and 8-bit color images. Figure 12.2 shows a photo before and after the information was hidden by changing the least significant bits. This was a color image but is reproduced as black and white in the book. Even in this format, it is easy to see the significant distortion introduced by the steganography process.

The errors were introduced because of the structure of the palette of 256 colors used in the image. Figure 12.3 shows a black and white representation of the 256 colors. Although the hue information is missing, you can easily see that many colors with a different level of saturation are next to each other. Changing the least significant bits will flip colors between adjacent pairs.

Page 132 shows some of the basic ways to sort a color palette.

Figure 12.2. A picture of Romana Machado before and after changing the least significant bits to add more information. (Photo by David Erck.)

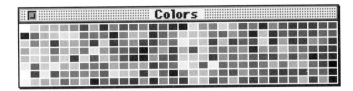

Figure 12.3. The palette of 256 colors used in Figure 12.2. Notice that many adjacent colors are obviously very different, even in this black and white representation.

Machado's second program, EzStego, tries to solve this problem by sorting the palette and placing similar colors near each other. This sorting routine is based upon the traveling salesman problem, a problem which asks for the best order to visit a list of n cities so as to minimize the traveling distance. In this version in color space, the object is to find the best order of the colors in the palette so that the total of the "distances" between colors is minimized. The "distance" between two colors, (r_1, g_1, b_1) and (r_2, g_2, b_2) is defined to be:

$$\sqrt{(r_1 - r_2)^2 + (g_1 - g_2)^2 + (b_1 - b_2)^2}$$

Solving the traveling salesman problem is normally considered to be a difficult problem because there is no known way to find the best answer without examining many of the possible solutions. This number usually grows exponentially as the number of colors or cities increases. Machado chooses a basic sorting algorithm to rebuild the palette. The procedure scans through the list of colors and chooses the optimal one to insert into the list at each step.

She also offers a Web-based version which allows anyone with a browser to process the data remotely at her site. See `http://www-.stego.com`. It's quite nice.

S-Tools

One of the best programs for hiding information in files is Andrew Brown's S-Tools.[1] The program will hide information in the least significant bits of either audio files or images. The latest version at this

---

[1]`asb@nexor.co.uk` or Andrew Brown, 28 Ashburn Drive, Wetherby, West Yorkshire, LS22 5RD, UK.

writing is version 4.0 and it runs only on Windows 95 and Windows NT machines. The earlier versions ran on Windows 3.1 and also contained a module that would hide information in the unallocated blocks of a disk.

The program will also add some simultaneous encryption to ensure that the data is doubly secure and also less obtrusive. Encrypted files often look more random and thus do a better job of appearing to be noise. S-Tools offers encryption with most of the major algorithms (IDEA, DES) and also implements many of their block chaining methods. The first block is padded with random noise to ensure that the data is even harder to discover.

The image padding part of S-Tools supports two different types of image files: 24-bit and 8-bit. The 24-bit images get new data added to the least significant bit of the red, green, and blue components. This process works quite well with 24-bit color images and the results are not obtrusive. The least significant bits of many scanned images are often close to random already so there may be little statistical effect in many cases.

Andrew Brown points out, quite correctly, that 24-bit images stand out especially on the Internet because most people use 8-bit images to save space. This is becoming less and less common on computers themselves because most machines now come with capable video cards with enough video memory to display 24-bit color all of the time. The 24-bit stigma will continue to apply to images from the Net because the bandwidth limitations will continue to force Web page designers to choose compact formats as much as possible.

The program uses a novel approach for constructing 8-bit images with steganographic data. It begins with an image and converts it into a 24-bit image. Then it tries to hide information by flipping the least significant bit. This will increase the number of colors in the image. There may be 256 colors in the initial image. Flipping the least significant bits may increase the number of colors by a factor of two, three, or even eight depending upon the image and the data being fed into it. This occurs because there may be many pixels that share the same color in the 256-color image. Each of these pixels will get a different 3 bits mixed into it. There are eight possible changed versions of this color, and the number of possible ones that occur in the tagged image will depend upon the tagging data and the composition of the image itself. It is not uncommon for the full 2048 colors to be present in the final image.

If there are 2048 colors in the tagged image, then an 8-bit image file can't be used to hold the data without losing some of the tagging information. A standard color reduction algorithm will blur pixels together and dump the information. S-Tools solves this problem by using a color reduction algorithm *before* adding the tagging bits. For instance, it will take the 256 initial colors and try to find 64 colors that best approximate these 256 colors. Then it will add in the tagging data and count the final colors. If it is lucky, there will be less than 256 and the result can be stored in an 8-bit file.

If too many colors are still left in the image, S-Tools begins a limbo game. It keeps trying to reduce the number of initial colors again and again. It may need to go as low as 32 initial colors if the colors are well distributed throughout the image.

The color reduction algorithm is always important in this case. S-Tools uses Paul Heckbert's [Hec82] to cut the number of colors. This algorithm tries to partition the color space into relatively equal amounts of space. That is, it begins with a $256 \times 256 \times 256$ element cube and then it recursively sub-divides it until there are 256 total boxes that represent the colors.

Heckbert developed the algorithm to combat the problems he noted with "popularity" algorithms that would clump together nearby colors until there were only 256 total colors left. Each of these clumps would be represented by one color, usually the average. This works well for tight clumps because there isn't much variation between values in the clump, but it can be problematic for the larger clouds. The average of these colors may not be visually close to any of the colors in the cloud, making everyone unhappy.

Heckbert's algorithm will subdivide boxes instead of clumping together colors. At each step the "largest" box is cut in half. This essentially guarantees that each box will be roughly the same size. There won't be a set of tight clumps and diffuse clouds of colors. Here's the algorithm explained:

- Start with all colors in one $256 \times 256 \times 256$ box.

- Repeat this inner loop for subdividing one box until the desired number of boxes are found:

  - Find the "largest" box. Heckbert does this by finding the "largest" dimension of the cloud of colors in each box. That is, he finds the minimum and maximum values for the red, green, and blue components for each color in the box.

– Convert the maximum and minimum values in each box into the dimensions for the box. This may be done by simple subtraction or it could be done in a more sophisticated way by computing the difference in luminance.

– Find the longest dimension of all of the boxes. Split this box. Heckbert offers two possible methods: find the median color along this dimension or simply split the box in half along this dimension. The median color solution will do a better job of placing an equal number of colors in each box. The geometric solution will do a better job of keeping the boxes equal in volume.

• At this point there are n boxes and a representative color for each box must be found. S-Tools implements three possible solutions for this: 1) find the center of the box, 2) average the colors in the box, or 3) average all of the pixels in the box. (1) and (3) are close to each other and provide a good geometric solution. (2) is the best choice if there is a tight clump inside a box that is not near the center.

This algorithm clearly does a better job of dealing with an image that may have many colors clustered around and a few in the outer regions. This may be common in images of faces. Heckbert offers the analogy that clustering color reduction algorithms are similar to the House of Representatives in the U.S. Congress. The districts for each representative are drawn so that each district contains roughly the same number of people. Heckbert's algorithm, on the other hand, is similar in spirit to the Senate which has two representatives from each state.

Regardless of the color reduction algorithm, there are several problems with the S-Tools approach to inserting data in 8-bit images. When the software is finished, the colors will be clustered in eight little color blocks around the initial colors. The process of reducing the initial colors and then adding the tagging data ensures that the final image will have about 32 to 60 clusters of about five to eight colors. This may be visually pleasing, but it should be easy for an automatic program to detect. This behavior is unlikely to happen in normal pictures.

It is interesting to compare this approach to the sorted palette solution in Machado's EzStego. Machado's solution will work only with the original 256 colors in the image. This can be very destructive if two adjacent colors are not that close even after sorting. Changing the least significant bit will flip between them and this may introduce weird effects. This effect will not happen with Brown's S-Tools, but the cost is a palette with a weird structure.

The best solution may be some sort of mixture. First construct an optimal set of 128 boxes using Heckbert's reduction algorithm. Some of the boxes will have only one of the 256 initial colors. Other boxes will have more. Each box will contribute two colors to the final palette of 256 colors. If a box has two colors in it, add those two colors to the final palette. If a box has one, then add that color and the center of the box to the final palette. If there are more than two colors, then choose two either randomly or by choosing the two closest to the center. This solution will produce a palette with the largest possible fraction of the initial palette while still ensuring that the process of tagging the image will not swap vastly different colors. Naturally, this approach may also be somewhat statistically suspect if the pairs of colors in the palette are too near each other.

S-Tools and Sound Files

The S-Tools will also hide information in the least significant bits of WAV sound files common on the Windows platform. These may use either 8 or 16 bits to represent the intensity at each sampling moment. The data may also be encrypted before it is inserted into the file.

The S-Tools program was designed more as an instrument of privacy than a tool for defending copyright. When the tagging data is smaller than the space available in the least significant bits, S-Tools will use a pseudo-random number generator to choose the subset of bits that are changed. This means that a short tag will be spread out very thinly over an audio file. This means that the channel may be effectively destroyed by a simple editing operation. Even removing one sample from the beginning of the file ensures that the bit selection algorithm will choose the wrong bits.

The best solution for copyright protection with S-Tools is to hide the maximum size file. This will turn off the random bit selection and spread the data throughout the file. Another good solution is to add a fair amount of error correction and repeat the tagging message again and again. This will provide some resistance to editing.

Hiding Information in Unallocated Diskspace

An earlier version of S-Tools came with a program called st-fdd.exe that could hide information in the unallocated sections of either a floppy disk or a hard drive. This program does not work with Windows 95 or Windows NT because these operating systems prevent access to the raw disk sectors. If you run Windows 3.1, however, then the program may be useful. This allows you to tag individual disks with customized information that will not be apparent to the user.

The unallocated disk space is a potential gold mine, but it can be fragile. Any common user will not see any information present because the standard file operations don't see a file. If the block is not assigned to a particular file, then the basic disk operation won't even know it's there. This is great when someone is browsing, but it can be a disaster if someone writes a new file to disk. The basic disk routines are likely to simply write over the hidden data because they think that nothing is there.

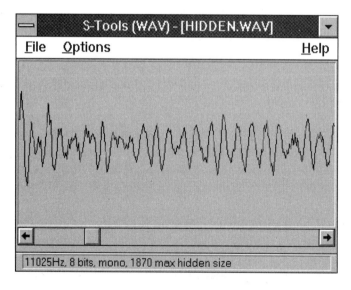

Figure 12.4. Here's the display window from st-wav.exe, the S-Tools program running on Windows 3.1. It will hide information in a WAV file. The program displays the changed parts of the waveform in red, but this detail is lost in a black and white book.

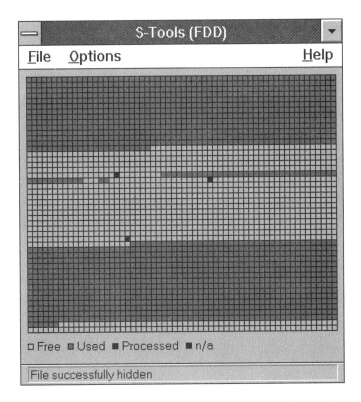

Figure 12.5. The main window from st-fdd.exe that shows the allocated sectors in red, the unallocated sectors in gray, and the ones that have been converted to hide information in yellow. This book, however, is printed in gray and the few yellow sections are almost indistinguishable from the gray.

The st-fdd.exe program is fairly clever. If you give it n bytes of data and there are m bytes of available unallocated disk space, then it will spread out the n bytes by using a pseudo-random number generator to choose disk blocks. The rest of the disk blocks can be overwritten with random noise to preserve the effect. The standard components of encryption algorithms are also available to simultaneously encrypt the information while storing it.

The header for the S-Tools contains the length of the file and the random number seed used to drive the block selection algorithm. This information is encrypted if an encryption algorithm is used and so you must have the key to even begin to recover the locations where the data may be.

Chapter 13

Original Conundrums

This chapter considers some of the legal questions created by the ease of replication in this electronic era.

Most people who are attracted to the techniques in this book are probably in the business of selling information. Some of the most interested are probably those who come from old-line publishing houses that built their business on the fact that the high cost of running a printing press was one of the best defenses against copyright infringement. The digital future with fast and easy replication is already a practical reality and many people are scared. Kids are making mix tapes, folks are duplicating movies, and electronic versions of Dilbert are flowing through the Internet non-stop. Copyright holders take one look at this and feel mugged by technology.

I think they're wrong. We're about to enter one of the greatest eras for growth in the creativity business ever. This will happen because the old forms of copyright protection (the high cost of a printing press or a television station) are disappearing and making it easier, cheaper, and safer to distribute creative information throughout the world. It won't be long before LA will engulf America and everyone has a script in their pocket and a sensitive little authentic riff on society in their heart. To paraphrase Richard Nixon, "We're all screenwriters now."

Many corporate leaders and their accountants may nod in agreement and then raise a very good objection, "Where will the money come from?" Many large, copyright-driven industries see the boom in digital computers as a explosion in high-tech burglar gear. Kids and people will be able to copy information galore without paying the person who sweated to create it. Why will people pay Time Warner when their buddy will send them a free copy they downloaded from the Internet? Is anyone going to pay for the limousines and helicopter rides for the corporate stars?

These are good questions, but the only real danger is that the big companies will take them so seriously that they'll get the governments to "do something about it." That something may be some legislation that would either cripple the ability of computers and videocassette recorders to make copies or it could be broader legislation that would expand the rights that corporations could hold. These ideas come floating out of big corporations now and it might not be long before one or two of them stick.

One good example was a recent attempt in the fall of 1996 by the World Intellectual Property Organization to create a new type of intellectual property for people who compile databases. In the past, some companies invested a great deal of time and energy creating vast stores of facts and data and made their money by selling portions of them that answered the questions from their clients. The only problem is that all of the facts are in the public domain so someone could simply "steal" their work by getting an electronic copy of the database.

A good example of this is the West corporation from Minnesota. It began collecting the opinions of U.S. judges and published them in books effectively creating a basis for the system of precedent that controls the legal system today. Some states and courts create their own collections of opinions, but many rely upon West to do the work.

The major problem for West, however, is that there is no copyright on any of the judicial opinions. They are produced by U.S. government employees working on the taxpayer's dime. The text falls into the public domain and anyone could start assembling their own database of opinions by copying West's editions.

The WIPO approached this problem by proposing a new type of database exemption. If you compiled your information in a database and you kept the database current, then you would have the right to sue anyone who tried to "steal" the information by downloading it. There would be, presumably, fair use exemptions for people who used an insignificant amount of the database. If someone wanted to create a competing database, however, they would need to research all of the facts on their own.

At first glance, this seems like a fair notion. The companies with a database often did put plenty of time and effort into collecting the facts. If someone comes along and accesses the database to collect the facts, they're cutting out the legwork and research time. It's not unlike a leech.

The real flaw is that it assumes that the database companies created their database out of thin air. This may be the case in some ground-breaking areas, but in most cases the database company stitched together their database by assembling snippets of other people's work. A drug company on the cutting edge may build up a database about their particular interest in a completely new discovery and this information would be completely new. But most other works depend upon collecting old and new.

Where does the database begin and end? Every database owner would like to believe that they own the facts in their database and everyone else should pay them for the pleasure of knowing those facts. In reality, many of those facts came from many different sources. Some of those sources may consider themselves a database. Is it fair, for instance, to interview the man on the street and then consider what he tells you to be part of your protected database? Didn't the facts come from the database in his mind? What if he was basing his opinions on what his wife said last night? Who came first?

Many database companies probably looked at the WIPO proposals as a just reward for their hard work, but they should consider how much harder it would make their work in the future. If they want to add more information to the database, will they need to pay huge fees to everyone in their path?

These are the types of problems that await the future as copyright holders come to grips with the temptation to control their work. Many feel that money will just come flooding in through the front door if they could only get the right legal protections for their work. They never recognize that the costs for acquiring information will also rise.

This is the main reason technical solutions are a better approach. Naturally, this opinion would make sense coming from the author of a book of technical solutions. But technical solutions can be flexible, inclusive, and more adaptable than legal solutions. A new law or regulation always comes with multiple meanings and this ambiguity can cause stress and arguments.

Legal solutions must be solved by the courts and the police. Arguing the details and splitting the hairs are outrageously expensive and barely affordable for all but the biggest corporations. Technical solutions can be modified on the fly. The copyright holders have a great stake in ensuring that the users can easily access the information and use it appropriately.

There is no easy way for me to justify my predictions, because they are only predictions. But I think that history is a good beginning. The world has seen an explosion of creativity from the invention of the moveable type printing press to today. A greater fraction of the population makes its living as storytellers, editors, presenters, or creative souls than ever before. In the 1940s, there may have been only 40 to 50 literary novels published in America. Today, there may be that many literary novels coming out of one publishing company alone. I think the new realm of fast and easy electronic reproduction will only continue this trend.

Coda

This book is, in many ways, a reincarnation of my earlier book *Disappearing Cryptography*. That book explored all of the ways to hide information from even being discovered. It carried with it a smell of radical libertarian cyberpunk because it gave many different techniques for preventing other people from even knowing that you're communicating with someone else. The technology in the book offered many people the promise that they could talk without being overheard by their government and, naturally, this notion could be worrisome to governments everywhere.

If that book was a Christmas card to anarchy, this book is nice wrapped gift for the prevailing social order. It offers copyright holders the ability to control their information as none have before. There is nothing really more Orwellian than tagging each document with a unique tag to track the flow of information through the world. The irony is that much of the technology is the same. You can use the solutions in this book to hide data from someone, whether that someone is a simpleton being tracked or a cybercop on the beat.

The greatest problem may be trying to make something out of this. A nihilist may simply conclude that the FBI, the Casa Nostra, the Crips, the police, the NSA, and the DOJ are all just gangs with their own rules of plunder. The algorithms in this book are just tools that you can use to your gang's advantage. Anyone who watched the scenes at Waco, Texas would feel this way.

But, I think there is another path that must be considered. The United States, unlike many countries, was conceived with liberty and justice as a stated goal. In this case, liberty and justice stand at odds with each other. Liberty proposes that everyone should be able to move information as they please. Any tagging or tracking will only serve the needs of an oppressor. But justice demands that people who produce valuable goods be compensated if they want to be. Free copying is just a tool for theft.

There may be no easy way to reconcile the two worlds, but I think that the old doctrine of fair use is an excellent beginning. Many people like to believe that cyberspace is a whole new world with entirely new rules, problems, and solutions. In practice, it's much the same as the regular world of paper and pencil, but the speeds and the economics are slighly different.

I think fair use can be applied very easily to the electronic world. Reasonably small parts of a piece should be easily replicated with few legal hassles. While the definition of "reasonable" will be subject to some debate, the overall concept can still be used.

People will continue to uncover some conundrums. Should it be legal, for instance, to simply copy the daily version of Dilbert to my home page? What if I used surreptitious schemes to simply edit Dilbert out of the syndicate's page? These questions will confound us, but there is no reason why the principle of fair use can't provide enough guidance.

Dan Wallach has amusing stories of his experiments with this on his home page.

For this reason, I hope that the techniques in this book are used with some care and caution. It would be easy to mandate some worldwide data tracking system that would open the door to the most Orwellian nightmares. Publishers and creative people have flourished where freedom was available and I hope that they'll recognize the danger in building up legal monuments to their creativity.

Appendix A

Permission

Many people putting together books are surprised that the rules of copyright prevent them from using other people's work. The law on copyright is far from clear. In order to raise the public's understanding of the subject, I asked a few simple questions of two of the most prominent intellectual property lawyers in the United States: Ed Rosenthal, a partner at the New York City law firm of Frankfurt, Garbus, Klein & Selz, P.C., and Max Waldbaum at the New York City law firm of Fried, Frank, Harris, Schriver & Jacobson.

Q. & A. with Ed Rosenthal

Ed Rosenthal is a partner at the New York City law firm of Frankfurt, Garbus, Klein & Selz, P.C., which specializes in copyright, trademark, and publishing counseling and litigation. (E-mail: erosenthal@fgks.com.) He represents several major publishers in New York City.

Q: What are the most important concepts that people have to look out for when considering whether they can use someone else's materials?
A: There are two critical concepts. First, copyright law does not protect facts or ideas; it only protects the way that those ideas are expressed. Second, there is a concept called fair use, which permits you, in certain circumstances, to use a portion of someone else's copyrighted work.

Q: How can you determine what is an idea and what is expression?
A: Sometimes it is a very difficult distinction, and there are many court decisions dealing with this subject. But much of the time, it is fairly straightforward. Anyone can write about a particular news event, or moment in history, or even a book or a movie. What you are not allowed to do is copy the words that someone else used, or even the specific order in which the other person has presented the ideas.
Q: Is it OK to paraphrase?
A: Not necessarily. Often when you paraphrase, you end up taking some of the original language and expression from the original. Also, you may run into the danger noted above about using the sequence of ideas presented in the original.
Q: Tell me about fair use.
A: Fair use is a concept that is defined in the copyright law. It is there to make sure that the public has an opportunity to review, criticize and discuss other people's expression in order to further the free marketplace of idea.
Q: Fair use is a difficult concept, isn't it?
A: It can be, depending upon the situation. The copyright statute sets forth four factors that courts look at to determine if the use of copyrighted material is fair. They are: 1) the purpose and character of the use (greater leeway is given if the use is for educational, rather than purely commercial purposes); 2) the nature of the copyrighted work (it is safer to use factual or historical works than it is to use fiction); 3) the amount of the copyrighted material used in relation to the copyrighted work as a whole; and 4) the effect of the use on the potential market for the copyrighted work.
Q: Are some factors more important than others?
A: Many courts look especially hard at the fourth factor. If the use is going to harm the copyright owner's economic interest in his or her work, it is going to be hard to prove that the use is fair.
Q: Aren't there some hard and fast rules, such as that it is OK to use 150 words from a book or four lines of a poem or eight bars of music?
A: Absolutely not! There are no magic rules at all, and believing that there are often gets people into trouble. The number of words you can use, or lines from a poem, or bars from a musical composition depends upon all of the circumstances. If you are writing scholarly literary criticism of another person's work, you have a lot more leeway than if you are creating a television commercial.
Q: What is public domain material?

A: Some materials have fallen into the public domain because the copyright has expired or because certain formalities have not been complied with. Also, some kinds of materials, such as official publications by the United States government, are not protected.

Q: How do you know if something is in the public domain?

A: If a work was published in the United States more than 75 years ago, it probably is in the public domain. But you should check with an expert because the law varies from country to country and because there have been many recent changes. For example, under current law in the United States, works created by an individual are protected for 50 years after death. And this law may soon change to comport with a recent trend in other countries toward making the term life plus 70 years.

Q: Sometimes you see that a work has a symbol or other notice of copyright. What is the meaning of this?

A: Until fairly recently, works that did not include a copyright notice (©) could fall into the public domain. That is no longer true and you should not assume that a document or other material that does not have a notice is not protected by copyright.

Q: Can you fairly use part of an image, say, by cropping out the face?

A: No. First, it is important to keep in mind that any duplication or reproduction of the original may be a copyright infringement. So even the act of photocopying or scanning the original in order to be able to crop or manipulate it may be illegal. Moreover, it can be copyright infringement to use someone else's work to create your own, even if no one looking at your work would recognize the original.

Q: Are there certain kinds of works that are particularly dangerous to use?

A: Yes. It is very difficult to establish fair use of a photograph, unless your use is actually to criticize the photo. Another danger area is music. There a couple of reasons for this. First of all, use of a fairly small amount of the original may constitute a significant taking. Moreover, you may have to worry about more than one copyright owner. For example, you may have to worry about the performer/record label that owns rights in the recording that you are using as well as the person who wrote the music. Depending upon the work and the kind of use you are making, there can be other issues as well.

Q: What about sampling of music? Has anything ever been resolved on this issue?

A: The general trend in the music industry today is to obtain permission before sampling someone else's work. There have only been a few court cases, but the person sampling another's music has tended to lose.

Q: Most publishers have permissions departments. How should they be approached?

A: If you are talking about a request to use a short quotation from a book, many publishers will be willing to grant permission for a small price. Publishers are more likely to be concerned about uses of their works electronically, such as on the Internet, because there is a danger that the material may be further reproduced and used without permission.

Q: If a publisher requests payment for using some section, is there room for bargaining?

A: In theory there should be. It may depend upon whom you are dealing with at the publisher and whether that person has been given any discretion to negotiate. If you find you are having difficulty, you may want to try to reach someone in the legal department of the publishing company.

Q: Is it possible to negotiate for different levels of rights for reprinting something?

A: Yes. The amount that you will need to pay for permission may depend on a number of factors, including how much you are using and what kind of use you are going to make. For example, it is likely to cost less to obtain permission to use a line from a poem in your book than if you wanted to use it in a television commercial. The cost also may depend the term of the permission (i.e., the length that you will be using it, the territorial extent of the use and the kind of media).

Q: What about reproducing databases?

A: Because, as described above, facts are not protectable, no one can own the facts that go into making a database. It is, however, possible to own rights in the choice of which facts are selected for inclusion as well as the order and arrangement of the material. In other words, be very careful before you reproduce someone else's database.

Q: Are there other dangers that you would like to point out?

A: Operators of online services as well as chat rooms and bulletin boards can be at risk if someone else uses your service to permit the unauthorized use of someone else's copyrighted materials. There have been a number of cases, with varying degrees of success, against online services, bulletin board operators and others claiming that they have facilitated copyright infringement. If you are aware, for example, that someone else is using your bulletin board to make copyrighted material, including such items as photographs, music or even short sound files, you could be held liable.

Q: Do you have any more suggestions?

A: This is a very complicated area of the law, and an area that is being forced to deal with rapidly changing technology. Many people have serious misconceptions about what they can and cannot do.

Q. & A. with Max Waldbaum

Mr. Waldbaum is a senior litigation partner at Fried, Frank, Harris, Shriver & Jacobson, One New York Plaza, New York, New York 10004, Tel. 212-859-8381. He is the head of the Intellectual Property Group, a member of the Patent Bar and has practiced in the areas of patent, trademark and copyright litigation since 1970. He received his bachelor of science degree in electrical engineering from Rutgers University (1964), a masters of science in electrical engineering from the Moore School of Electrical Engineering, University of Pennsylvania (1966), and his law degree from New York University (J.D., cum laude, Order of the Coif, Salutatorian) (1970). He is a member of the bars of State of New York, the United States District Courts for the Southern District of New York, Eastern District of New York, Eastern District of Michigan, Western District of New York, United States Court of Appeals for the Second Circuit, Third Circuit, Federal Circuit and Supreme Court of the United States.

Mr. Waldbaum is President of the Federation Internationale des Conseils en Propriete Industrielle (FICPI), U.S. Group. It is an organization of 3,500 intellectual property lawyers all of the free profession (law firms). He is currently a member of the Board of Directors of the International Trademark Association (INTA) where he has chaired committees on counterfeiting and education for the last seven years. He has lectured and written widely on intellectual property issues and is currently the co-author of the yearly updated publication "Acquiring and Protecting Intellectual Property Rights" with Donald Chisum (Matthew Bender). Mr. Waldbaum has litigated in all sciences in patent disputes, been involved in major trademark litigations and has had many substantial copyright matters, including a wide variety of software related issues.

Q: "Fair use" is a difficult term for many people to define. Do you have any suggestions?

A: The basic way to look at whether a use is "fair" is to look at the actual product used and the motivation of the user. If the motivation is for teaching, criticism, comment, a reporting of the news, or for academic research, there will be a heavy burden put on the copyright owner to claim that there should be a copyright infringement found and that the use was not fair. The initial burden will always be on the user to show fair use. I think that once you look at the motivation behind the user you will normally obtain your answer as to whether the use was fair. Although, fair use can typically be commercial use.

Analysis of the actual use, how many pages of a book are used, where the use is circulated and how the market is affected come into play, for the most part, as secondary factors. Clearly if a use is, for example, satire, but there is a heavy commercial value because of the person who is using the material, then the question shifts to whether the satire is fair satire protected by the First Amendment or satire which uses the fame of the person or product subject to the satire and thus potentially improper. There have been many bad cases in the area of satire because of the local concerns in the federal district in which the case is brought. The best example is the near-pornographic satire of the L.L. Bean catalog where the action was brought in Maine. It was more the protection of a public icon and major corporation representing the state of Maine than a question of whether satire was covered by the First Amendment. That issue got lost in the self-protection mechanism of a provincial court.

If motivation doesn't answer the question, then you must look to how much the user has affected the value of the copyright for its originator or creator. It may require an analysis of the potential market value of the copyrighted work if the above analysis doesn't immediately answer the question.

In all, it is a balancing of the motivation of the user, the amount copied and the clear harm to the creator or originator in complete disregard of his rights by the user. Every case has a theme and the theme can determine through its story the right or wrong of the fairness of the use. But the answer rarely lies in the use of calipers to measure how much of a product was taken.

The cases involving researchers who take publications and store them on their shelves as permanent personal libraries (which is a violation in the Second Circuit) and university professors who copy at will articles at full length for their courses and students (which also is a violation) are extreme cases of recognizing the value lifted from a copyright owner. As you go down in gradations from those examples, things become fuzzy and lawyers can best answer the question from a close analysis of the cases.

One of the problems with whether a use is "fair" or not is how much money is involved in litigating the issues. If it is a small amount, it is not worth the candle and the issue never gets appropriately resolved. A good way to resolve a fair use question is to work directly with the alleged infringer to determine his motivation and create an environment that will either end his usage or allow you to test the use in a setting that you have made more clear by actions of confrontation.

Q: Are there any major court cases that can act as guideposts?

A: Yes, there are quite a few. *Feist Publications v. Rural Telephone Service Co.*, 499 U.S. 340 (1991) set the modern day standard for originality versus fair use for compilations. It indicated that a telephone directory, i.e., white pages, must embody some degree of original expression either in selection arrangement or coordination and the copyright protection extends only to such expression not to the underlying data or non-expressive elements. Id. at 351. The court in Feist found no originality and thus no protection. *Feist* is also important because it rejects the "sweat of the brow" justification as no longer relevant to an inquiry of originality in copyright cases. See for example *Rand McNally and Co. v. Fleet Management System Inc.*, 600 F.Supp. 933 (N.D. Ill. 1984). (Compilations of mileage data were copyrightable.)

The court in Feist further noted that in a compilation where an author adds "no written expression but rather lets the facts speak for themselves, the expressive element is more elusive. The only conceivable expression is the manner in which the compiler has selected and arranged the facts . . . . No matter how original the format, however, the facts themselves do not become original through association." *Id.* at 349.

In most digital communications, such as financial information or data gathering for any purpose, such raw facts, it appears from Feist, may be used by others without compensation. Although this appears unfair considering the compiler's labor has borne fruit that is not compensated, Feist indicates the result is just because it is the "means by which copyright advances the progress of science and art." *Id.* at 350.

As for the fair use or protectability for mathematical constants used in copyrighted computer programs, they were held to be unprotectable as facts even though the designers claimed that the constants had been determined by engineers who gathered data, compared and interpreted all results and then came up with numbers that in their opinions were representative of the group. *Gates Rubber Co. v. Bando Chemical Industries, Ltd.*, 9 F.3d 823, at 843, fn. 20 (10th Cir. 1993). As I noted above it is very difficult to claim protection for such mathematical equations or constants.

Fair use is also limited by protections given to compilers who choose to exclude certain types of information and include certain other headings and arrangements that are unique. In *Key Publications Inc. v. Chinatown Today Publishing*, 945 F.2d 509, 512 (2nd Cir. 1991), a publisher of a business directory for New York City's Chinese-American community was able to have a court conclude a directory was original (even though there was a finding of no infringement). The conclusion was based upon the plaintiff's selection and arrangement of listings. This included the arrangement of headings that were unique and the exclusion of certain information. In *Key* the court found no infringement because the competing directory used the underlying facts only. *Id.* at 520.

Of course, under what is known as the merger doctrine, data is not protected if the idea behind the work is merged with its expression. That is, when there is only one way to express an idea there will be no enforceability and, consequently, fair use, because the courts will not allow the effective monopolization of an idea. *Kregos v. Association Press*, 937 F.2d 700, 705 (2nd Cir. 1991). (Baseball statistic tabulations.) In *Kern River Gas Transmission Co. v. Coastal Corp.*, 899 F.2d 1458 (5th Cir. 1990), cert. denied 498 U.S. 952 (1990), the court refused to grant copyright protection for maps depicting the proposed location of a pipeline as there was only one approved route and a map was the only way to communicate that route.

Even though a use is of a commercial character, that does not presumptively bar a finding of fairness. *Sony Corp. of America v. University City Studios Inc.*, 464 U.S. 417, 451 (1983). Where, of course, entire articles are photocopied and retained in the files of an engineer for future use that will be found to be not fair use. *American Geophysical Union, et al. v. Texaco Inc.*, 60 F.3d 913 (2d Cir. 1994). Fair use is more easily found when factual works are copied as opposed to creative works. *Campbell v. Acuff-Rose Music Inc.*, 114 S.Ct. 1164 (1994).

In *Maxtone-Graham v. Burtshaell,* 803 F.2d 1253 (2nd Cir. 1986), cert. denied, 481 U.S. 1059 (1987), the question was whether a later author who published a book which quoted extensively from interviews which were set forth in a prior book was found to be a copyright infringer. The court in Burtshaell found that the nature of the work weighed in favor of a fair use due to the essentially factual nature of the previous work which is mainly made up of interviews. The court found that "subsequent authors may rely more heavily on such work". *Id.* at 1263. This is to be compared with the works copied in Texaco above where they were articles in scientific journals, that is, creative and original expression, albeit concerning factual matters and should be afforded more protection than mere factual compilations.

One of the guideposts is to determine whether an implied license is created by the manner in which the copyright owner distributes the work and intends the work to be used by others. For example, when a company presents data to the public in a magazine such as a weekly publication and expects the data to be used by people in particular industries, it can be fairly argued that there is an implied license to use that data even though the original work was copyrighted and only paid for once. This non-exclusive license may arise by implication where the creator of a work at defendant's request hands it over intending the defendant to copy and distribute it. *Effects Associates Inc. v. Cohen,* 908 F.2d 555 (9th Cir. 1990). In Effects the subject matter at issue was special effects footage for incorporation into a horror movie where the only purpose the parties could have contemplated was distribution and copying. A license to incorporate footage into the movie derived from the creation and physical transfer for commission of that footage. In *McClean Associates v. William M. Mercer-Mitinger-Hanson,* 952 F.2d 769 (3rd Cir. 1991) (quoting Effects, supra) the court found an implied non-exclusive license for a computer company to use software developed by an independent contractor expressly for the benefit of one certain client. Thus, the license is implied where one party for consideration intentionally offers and delivers copyrightable material to another party. Common sense dictates that the material would be worthless without the implied, non-exclusive license.

With respect to fair use and enjoyment by third parties of copyrighted information, one should always keep in mind the exhaustion doctrine: Once a product is licensed or sold, the control of the exclusive rights in the copyright has been exhausted. Similar to trademark law, the doctrine of exhaustion precludes the original owner of an intellectual property right from exercising control over that right after it has been injected into the stream of commerce as long as no likelihood of confusion exists (trademark concept). *Matrix Essentials Inc. v. Emporium Drug Mart Inc.*, 988 F.2d 587 (5th Cir. 1993).

The exhaustion doctrine avoids abusing intellectual property law for purposes that extend beyond the law's intent. This doctrine applies as well to patents, trademarks and copyrights. The sale of the copyrighted work "exhausts the monopoly in that article" and the intellectual property owner cannot "control the use or disposition of the article" (patent in question in this case, *United States v. Univis Lens Co. Inc.*, 316 U.S. 241, 250 (1942).

The final legal principle that one should consider in analyzing guideposts is whether there should be a consideration of preemption by patent law as to any alleged copyright protection. *Bonita Boats Inc. v. Thundercraft Boats Inc.*, 489 U.S. 141, 152 (1989). So one has to come to the question of whether the data being communicated is protected as invention. If that is true, depending on the information, it may have been properly subject to patent and therefore preempted by congressionally announced policies.

Q: Can you fairly use part of an image, say, by cropping out the face?

A: Yes and no. If the image sufficiently presents the creative expression as set forth in the image before cropping out then there would be no fair use and it would be a commercial taking of the creative expression. If a new and different expression occurs which is substantially unrelated to the original image then an argument could possibly be made for fair use and new creative expression. The problem here is that it would probably be looked at as a derivative work and as a derivative work you are always subject to the argument of infringement on the prior work.

If the suggestion is an image that includes an entire picture including one face which you crop out, then it doesn't seem to matter if just the face is cropped out, the rest of the expression is completed. For example, putting a MAD Magazine (Alfred E. Newman) face on President Clinton in a well known photograph of the president. A typical example is the cropping of body parts such as the example in TV Guide where Oprah Winfrey had her face put on the body of someone else to create a better image. These situations are very difficult because they create a different look to an individual and gets into the right of publicity and the potential for harming the reputation of famous persons.

If the image suggested to be cropped is just an unknown photographic or painted image, or even digital image on a computer (more likely) then the question remains what is left of the creative expression once the cropping takes place. It goes to 17 U.S.C. §107(2) as to the nature of the copyrighted work if a new and very different work has been created. A further issue is under 17 U.S.C. §107(3)—the substantiality of the portion used to create the new creative expression and how new is this expression. All these issues are heavily fact intensive.

Q: Musical quotation is a big battleground. Can someone safely quote sections of music?

A: This has been a very much litigated question. The problem has to do with the originality of the parts of the music which are taken. As an example, I can recall being asked to judge whether there was appropriate copyright infringement where the first portions of a musical composition (rap) were simply the scratching of a record, such as improperly taking the needle off a phonograph and whether that "musical" taking was enough to create copyright infringement for future rap music where the only similarity was the scratching of the record to start the music. I felt then and I feel now that such a choice for copyright expression is de minimus and not subject to protection. The copyright owner/accuser went away quickly. They could never articulate a legitimate position.

There is presently litigation as to whether the copyrightability of the actual musical notes themselves (just the notes) in a collection for a player piano is subject to copyright protection. There seems to be a very good argument for no originality in the collection of those notes simply placed on a computer chip for presentation in a player piano. However, there is some case law (or indications) contrary.

The presentation of evidence is very important to show that the amount or quality of the musical information which is taken is substantial enough to be considered the taking of an original musical piece. There are some situations where the mere compilation of two or three notes is recognized immediately as the composition of something very famous, for example, the lead into Beethoven's 5th Symphony (four notes) or the chimes for the NBC peacock (three notes). Presently there is litigation pending in the United States Patent and Trademark Office on the appropriateness of the sound of a Harley-Davidson motorcycle. If Harley-Davidson is correct, no one can appropriate any part of that sound that substantially gives the impression of a Harley. The key to these questions regarding musical note-taking as copyright infringement are answered by (1) the nature of the work, that is, whether it is recognizable to a consumer population that the music is very recognizable, original and has commercial value and (2) whether there is a substantial taking in terms of amount or quantification to allow one to conclude that it should be considered copyright infringement. In this regard, musical notes should be considered similar to any other types of data in digitized or other format and analyzed in just the same way. Further, there is clearly a trademark/identification of source issue here as well.

Whether someone can safely quote sections of music depends in large part on the amount they wish to quote and the reasons they wish to quote such music. If it is for criticism, commentary or news reporting then it can be done as fair use. If it is for commercial purposes then the question is has something original been quoted (and it probably is since it's being quoted) which gives no safety net to the user. The answer is simply similar to any other copyrighted material and the commercial versus fair use of that material, purpose and motivation and the effect on the potential market for the music and its value.

Q: Getting permission for reproducing a package is often required by publishers. Is there a threshold that turns a permissible quote into a passage that requires a release?

A: I think so. The solution turns on the substantiality or quantification of the permissible quote. Reproducing a package indicates that there is going to be a commercial purpose for material from various publications. That being so, although all commercial uses are not necessarily not fair uses, there is a burden to be carried by the user to indicate that the use is fair. You have to once again go through the different factors which are fact intensive where the first factor, the purpose and character of the use, will probably play a dominant role in a conclusion as to whether the use was fair.

Q: Most publishers have permissions departments. How should they be approached?

A: Cautiously and with knowledge of the particular publisher's characteristics concerning use by third parties. If you show regard for the copyrighted work and indicate some valuable purpose which perhaps will enhance or add value (money, etc.) to the original work, then you might receive the right reaction for your request. There should be no reason to act in disregard or neglect with respect to such permissions department or with reckless abandon. These departments are fully aware of the rights of their authors and creators and should be given deference. You should also have a working knowledge of whether the particular publisher you are about to communicate with takes aggressive stances (by knowledge of past litigations) with respect to third party users.

Q: If a publisher requests payment for using some section, is there room for bargaining?

A: It is often possible to negotiate a proper payment because the use is always fact intensive. Unlike when you are dealing with the Commerce Clearing House (CCH) or ASCAP typically you can make your own deal for the particular purpose for which you are intending usage. This is true, for example, with the Software Publishers Association (SPA).

Q: Is it often possible to negotiate for different levels of rights for reprinting something?

A: I think this is true because the different levels of rights requested normally have different value. Certainly if you are asking for exclusive rights, you should expect to be paying more dearly. Also if you are asking to reprint important (high commercial value) publication information or data, you should expect to be paying a substantial price. This is also true with respect to reprinting a data sheet if you have many members of your company that want to separately analyze the data. Many of the data originating companies are taking very high exposure positions on the need to gain extra income from copying reprinted information. Many times negotiation can allow for little or no payment at all where the reprinting benefits both the user and the copyright owner. This may be true for a commercial printing which by technical definition would be outside the definition of fair use but still beneficial to the copyright owner.

Q: Any final comments?

A: The creation and transmission of information digitally with respect to any subject matter will be treated under standard copyright analysis. Although the forms and formats to be used will be new and, typically, there will be those who argue that there are new public policy reasons as for lesser or greater protection for these new transmissions, history dictates that the same rules and regulations will apply. The same standards for patentability and copyrightability will be applicable. There, of course, as with all new information transfer, will be a shakeout period where there will be varying positions but ultimately there will be a standardization which looks very much like what we lawyers have been doing all along. This will be true for electronic banking, encryption, data transfer, financial analysis and anything else digitally transmittable.

Appendix B

Important Patents

The U.S. Patent system is often a good source of clear descriptions of important technology because inventors often seek protection from infringement. Not all of the best technology is found here because some businesses may choose to keep technology secret. Also, some ideas may not be found by searching the body of outstanding patents because not all ideas are patentable for a number of different reasons. In any case, the patent office often takes one to three years to process patents so there is always some delay between the time that an invention is created and the time that the public can learn about it from the patent office.

This list of patents is not meant to be either comprehensive or complete. Searching the patent office can be compared to following a tree. Each new patent can lead you off down different paths and different classifications. If you plan to file a patent, you should start your own search and use your own invention to prune your search.

The patents in this section are largely taken from the U.S. Classification sections of 380-054 and 380-004.

This section reproduces the abstracts to the patents verbatim. The data was gathered from IBM's free patent search site on the Internet. The grammar and spelling errors are printed without correction because it is not clear who introduced them into the text. It may have been the patent applicant who never completely corrected all typos. Or it could have been the patent office transcribing it. Or it could have been IBM trying to track the flow of their data. Who knows?

5530759   Color correct digital watermarking of images
Gordon W. Braudaway, Karen A. Magerlein, and Frederick C. Mintzer

A system for placing a visible "watermark" on a digital image is disclosed, wherein an image of the watermark is combined with the digital image. The pixels of the watermark image are examined, and for each pixel whose value is not a specified "transparent" value, the corresponding pixel of the original image is modified by changing its brightness but its chromaticities. This results in a visible mark which allows the contents of the image to be viewed clearly, but which discourages unauthorized use of the image.

5488664   Method and apparatus for protecting visual information with printed cryptographic watermarks
Adi Shamir

A method and device for protecting visual information against unauthorized access and modification using a printed cryptographic watermark includes printing a first array of shapes on a first sheet of material to be protected and printing a second array of shapes on a second sheet of material, which is transparent so as to form a developer for developing a watermark encoded in a combination of the first and second arrays of shapes. The watermark is encoded by preparing each array using black and white pixels. Each pixel, which may be a square, rectangle, circle, hexagon or other shape, is split into first and second collections of subpixels, the first collection of subpixels appearing in the first array of shapes and the second collection of subpixels appearing in the second array of shapes. When the transparent second sheet of material is positioned directly on top of the first sheet of material with the second array of shapes aligned with the first array of shapes, the first sheet of material may be viewed through the transparent second sheet of material. In this manner, the encoded watermark, which was not visible in either one the two individually, becomes visible. Additionally, a first image may be encoded in the first sheet, a second image may be encoded in the second sheet, and the watermark may be viewed as a third image that is visible in the combination of the first and second sheets.

5003600   Diffraction gratings used as identifying markers
Vance A. Deason and Michael B. Ward

A finely detailed diffraction grating is applied to an object as an identifier or tag which is unambiguous, difficult to duplicate, or remove and transfer to another item, and can be read and compared with prior readings with relative ease. The exact pattern of the diffraction grating is mapped by diffraction moire techniques and recorded for comparison with future readings of the same grating.

Video Copy Protection

5583936   Video copy protection process enhancement to introduce horizontal and vertical picture distortions
Peter Wonfor, Alistair Knox, Jeremy Corcoran, John Ryan, and Ronald Quan

Enhancements to a video anticopying process that causes an abnormally low amplitude video signal to be recorded on an illegal copy. The enhancements in one version introduce into the overscan portion of the television picture, just prior to the horizontal or vertical sync signals but in active video, a negative going waveform that appears to the television receiver or videotape recorder to be a sync signal, thereby causing an early horizontal or vertical retrace. One version provides (in the right overscan portion of the picture), a checker pattern of alternating gray and black areas which causes the TV set on which the illegal copy is played to horizontally retrace earlier than normal in selected lines with a consequential horizontal shift of the picture information on those lines. This substantially degrades picture viewability. In another version a gray pattern at the bottom overscan portion of the picture causes vertical picture instability. In another version selected horizontal sync signals are narrowed, causing irregular vertical retraces. Also provided is apparatus for removing or attenuating these enhancements from the video signal, to allow copying.

5574787   Apparatus and method for comprehensive copy protection for video platforms and unprotected source material
John O. Ryan

A video recording platform prevents both analog and digital copying of copy protected material. The platform may input and output both analog and digital video signals. At said analog input, a detector detects conventional copy protection in the analog input video, and in response disables recording thereof. At the digital input, a first detector detects a copyright signature present in the input material and in response prevents recording. A specially adapted video recorder, playback device or set top decoder copy protects video source material which has a copyright signature. A copyright signature is provided in a predetermined location in said video signal to be protected. The video recorder, playback device, or set top decoder upon detection of the copyright signature on its input or at playback, modifies the output standard (NTSC) video signal with a conventional copy protection process and the digital output with a new copyright signature. The input digital signal may contain a scrambling of the digital video signal in addition to the copy protection signature. In addition, an authenticating signature may be added to the digital video signal and detected as part of the copy protection process. As part of the copy protection, a television receiver includes a copy protection and descrambling system.

5513260 Method and apparatus for copy protection for various recording media
John O. Ryan

A method and apparatus for copyright protection for various recording media such as compact discs (CDs) uses a combination of symmetrical and asymmetrical data encryption to permit the player to handle either copy-protected or non-copy-protected media, in a manner that is extremely difficult to compromise. Coupled with the combination of encrypting methods, an Authenticating Signature is recorded on the media only when copy-protection is required. The nature of this Authenticating Signature is such that it will not be transferred to illicit copies made on CD recorders. When either an original protected or an original non-protected disk is played, the presence or absence of the Authenticating Signature causes the player to correctly decrypt the program data. All original CDs therefore play normally. When a copy of a non-protected CD is played, the absence of the Authenticating Signature also causes the player to correctly decrypt the program data. However, when a copy of a protected CD is played, the absence of the Authenticating Signature causes the player to generate false data which prohibits the disk from playing normally.

5418853 Apparatus and method for preventing unauthorized copying of video signals
Keiji Kanota, Hajime Inoue, and Yukio Kubota

In a digital video tape recorder (VTR) which reproduces digital video and audio signals from a magnetic tape, a copy protect bit in the reproduced digital video signal is detected, and on the basis of the copy protect bit, a code is generated and inserted into the vertical blanking interval of the reproduced video signal. When a video signal (which may be in analog or digital form) having the code in the vertical blanking interval is received in a digital VTR, the code is detected and recording of the video signal and an associated audio signal is inhibited if the code indicates that the received video signal is copy protected.

5315448 Copy protection for hybrid digital video tape recording and unprotected source material
John Ryan

A hybrid digital/analog video recorder prevents both analog and digital copying. The recorder (including a digital tape deck) inputs and outputs both analog and digital video signals. At the analog input, a detector detects conventional copy protection in the analog input video, and in response disables recording thereof. At the digital input, a first detector detects anti-copy bits present in the input material and in response prevents recording. A second bit detector detects serial copy prevention scheme bits, and in response adds an anti-copy bit to the input digital stream, preventing later copying of such material. When another bit detector detects anti-copy bits present in the playback digital data stream prior to conversion to analog, an analog copy protection signal modifies the output analog signal, inhibiting copying of the output signal. In another version, a specially adapted video recorder or playback device copy protects video source material which for technical reasons is not copy protectable. A copy protect "flag" is provided in a predetermined location in the video signal to be protected. The video recorder or playback device, upon detection of the flag at playback, modifies the output standard (NTSC) video signal with a conventional copy protection process.

5251041 Method and apparatus for modifying a video signal to inhibit unauthorized videotape recording and subsequent reproduction thereof
Philip Young and Leonard Greenberg

A method and an apparatus which modifies a video signal such that a conventional video monitor reproduces a normal picture from the modified video signal, whereas a videotape recording of the modified video signal and subsequent playback thereof produces disturbances in the displayed picture. Predetermined portions of the video signal are identified and copy protection signals are added thereto. The signal mixing and delaying characteristics of a videotape recorder comb filter are exploited to modify, produce and relocate synchronization and burst interfering copy protection signals added to an original videotape recording.

4979210 Method and apparatus for protection of signal copy
Atsushi Nagata, Yutaka Uekawa, Takanori Senoo, and Kenichi Takahashi

An apparatus for the protection of signal copy for preventing unauthorized copying of music software such as records, compact discs and music tape by recording is arranged such that when recording audio signals on a medium, certain supplemental information is added to the audio signal to be recorded, and in the process of copying by reproducing this medium, when the supplemental signal is detected in the reproduced signal, the copying action is stopped to protect it from being copied.

5428598 Record carrier with copy bits
Hindrik Veldhuis, Rudolf Roth, and Jacobus Heemskerk

Methods of and information recording devices for recording and/or inhibiting recording of a signal including copy bits on a record carrier, and a record carrier including that signal. The signal has successive information frames including main data and subcode data. The subcode data of the information frames make up successive subcode frames having copy bits with logic values which alternate among the subcode frames in accordance with a predetermined pattern. Each subcode frame has at least one copy bit. In one of the embodiments, the signal is received and a determination is made whether to inhibit its recording on the basis of the predetermined pattern exhibited by the logic values of the copy bits contained in the subcode frames. In another embodiment the subcode frames are replaced by substitute subcode frames having copy bits with logic values which alternate among the substitute subcode frames in accordance with a selected pattern prior to recording of the signal. The predetermined and selected patterns are indicative of a particular characteristic of the main data (e.g., whether the main data is copy protected).

5179452 Method for producing copy protected recorded videotape having uncopyable vertical synchronizing signal partition
Yasunori Takahashi

A copy protection arrangement for pre-recorded videotape cassettes. The invention includes both a method of protecting and a protected videotape cassette. Copy protection is provided by recording on at least a portion of the original videotape a composite synchronizing signal including a vertical synchronizing pulse having a pulse width in the range of 1–20 micro-seconds and a pulse height discernible by a vertical synchronizing signal separating circuit of the television receiver. All other vertical synchronizing pulse in the vertical synchronizing signal partition, all the equalizing pulses in a equalizing signal partition following the vertical synchronizing signal partition and at least a part of the horizontal synchronizing pulses in a horizontal synchronizing signal partition following the equalizing signal partition in the composite synchronizing signal having respective pulse height less than a predetermined pedestal level of the synchronizing signals.

5073925 Method and apparatus for the protection of signal copy
Atsushi Nagata, Yutaka Uekawa, Takanori Senoo, and Kenichi Takahashi

An apparatus for the protection of signal copy for preventing unauthorized copying of music software such as records, compact discs and music tape by recording is arranged such that when recording audio signals on a medium, certain supplemental information is added to the audio signal to be recorded, and in the process of copying by reproducing this medium, when the supplemental signal is detected in the reproduced signal, the copying action is stopped to protect it from being copied.

5412718   Method for utilizing medium nonuniformities to minimize unauthorized duplication of digital information
Arcot D. Narasimhalu, Weiguo Wang, and Mohan S. Kankanhalli

The present invention is a method for preventing unauthorized copying and use of information which is stored on a storage medium and for restricting the use of such information to designated devices. Copy protection is achieved by generating a signature from a given storage medium. The signature is derived from an arbitrarily selected list of nonuniformities, uniformities and their attributes. The selected list may contain nonuniformities at any granularity level. As such, this signature is unique to a given storage medium in the same way fingerprints are unique to a human being. This signature is used to derive a key for encrypting the information on the storage medium. Any copying of the distribution information from one storage medium to another results in the mutation of the signature required to decrypt the information. Therefore, the present invention obviates the need for introducing artificial indica or requiring a special hardware subsystem for achieving a copy protection scheme. Restricting the usage of information on a distribution medium to a designated device is achieved by verifying the device ID (DID-D) of the device with the device ID (DID-S) stored in the distribution medium before the decryption and transfer of information are undertaken. Decryption of the information is accomplished by generating a key from both the signature of the distribution medium and the DID-S.

Appendix C

Bibliography

The field of copyright protection is a burgeoning business, but there is not much information in the general literature. One of the better collections of recent research is Ross Anderson's proceedings from the Information Hiding conference held in Cambridge in 1996 [And96]. The article by W. Bender, D Gruhl, N. Morimoto, and A. Lu [BGML96] is one of the better general introductions.

David Kahn's *Codebreakers* is an excellent survey of the history of cryptology [Kah67]. The book includes numerous descriptions of steganographic solutions like secret inks and microdots. The more recent articles about the history of cryptology can be found in the journal *Cryptologia*. He also wrote the introductory chapter to the proceedings from the Information Hiding conference and summarized the history of steganography.

Other more specific information can be found in these areas.

Error-Correcting Codes The chapter in this book cannot do justice to the wide field. There are many different types of codes with different applications. Some of the better introductions are [LJ83] and [Ara88]. There are many others.

Compression Algorithms Compression continues to be a hot topic and many of the latest books aren't current any longer. The best solution is to combine books like [Bar88a, Bar88b] with papers from the the proceedings from academic conferences like [Kom95].

[46-88]   NBS FIPS PUB 46-1. Data encryption standard. Technical report, National Bureau of Standards, U.S. Department of Commerce, Jan 1988.

[4677]   NBS FIPS PUB 46. Data encryption standard. Technical
            report, National Bureau of Standards, U.S. Department of
            Commerce, Jan 1977.

[AK91]   Dana Angluin and Michael Kharitonov. When won't
            membership queries help? In *Proceedings of the Twenty-
            Third Annual ACM Symposium on Theory of Computing*,
            pages 444–454. ACM Press, 1991. to appear in *JCSS*.

[And96]   Ross Anderson. *Information Hiding*. Springer-Verlag,
            Berlin, New York City, 1996.

[Ara88]   Benjamin Arazi. *A Commonsense Approach to the Theory of
            Error Correcting Codes*. MIT Press, Cambridge, MA, 1988.

[Arv91]   James Arvo. *Graphics Gems II*. Academic Press, San Diego,
            CA, 1991.

[Bar88a]   Michael F. Barnsley. Fractal modelling of real world im-
            ages. In Heinz-Otto Peitgen and Dietmar Saupe, editors,
            The Science of Fractal Images, chapter 5, pages 219–239.
            Springer-Verlag, 1988.

[Bar88b]   Michael F. Barnsley. *Fractals Everywhere*. Academic Press,
            San Diego, 1988.

[BGML96]   Walter Bender, D. Gruhl, N. Morimoto, and A. Lu. Tech-
            niques for data hiding. *IBM Systems Journal*, 35(3):313,
            1996.

[BLMO95]   Jack Brassil, Steve Low, Nicholas Maxemchuk, and Larry
            O'Gorman. Hiding information in document images. In
            *Proceedings of the 1995 Conference on Information Sciences
            and Systems*, March 1995.

[BM91]   S.M. Bellovin and M. Merritt. Limitations of the kerberos
            protocol. In *Winter 1991 USENIX Conference Proceedings*,
            1991.

[BO96]   Jack Brassil and Larry O'Gorman. Watermarking docu-
            ment images with bounding box expansion. In *Information
            Hiding, Lecture Notes of Computer Science (1174)*, New York,
            Heidelberg, 1996. Springer-Verlag.

[BS91a]   E. Biham and A. Shamir. Differential cryptanalysis of DES-like cryptosystems. In *Advances in Cryptology–CRYPTO '90 Proceedings*. Springer-Verlag, 1991.

[BS91b]   E. Biham and A. Shamir. Differential cryptanalysis of DES-like cryptosystems. *Journal of Cryptology*, 4(1):3–72, 1991.

[CKLS96]   Ingemar Cox, Joe Kilian, Tom Leighton, and Talal Shamoon. A secure, robust watermark for multimedia. In *Information Hiding, Lecture Notes of Computer Science (1174)*, New York, Heidelberg, 1996. Springer-Verlag.

[DS96]   Paul Davern and Michael Scott. Fractal based image steganography. In *Information Hiding, Lecture Notes of Computer Science (1174)*, New York, Heidelberg, 1996. Springer-Verlag.

[ed.92]   G.J. Simmons, ed. *Contemporary Cryptology: The Science of Information Integrity*. IEEE Press, Piscataway, NJ, 1992.

[ElG85]   T. ElGamal. A public-key cryptosystem and a signature scheme based on discrete logarithms. *IEEE Transactions on Information Theory*, IT-31(4), 1985.

[FS75]   R.W. Floyd and L. Steinberg. An adaptive algorithm for spatial gray scale. *Society for Information Displays*, 1975.

[FvDFH82]   James D. Foley, Andries van Dam, Steven K. Feiner, and John F. Hughes. *Computer Graphics Principles and Practice*. Addison-Wesley, Reading, MA, 1982.

[Gla90]   Andrew Glassner. *Graphics Gems*. Academic Press, San Diego, CA, 1990.

[Hec82]   Paul Heckbert. Color image quantization for frame buffer display. In *Proceedings of SIGGRAPH 682*, 1982.

[HU79]   John E. Hopcroft and Jeffrey D. Ullman. *Introduction to Automata Theory, Languages, and Computation*. Addison-Wesley, Reading, MA, 1979.

[Kah67]   David Kahn. *The Codebreakers*. Macmillan, New York City, 1967.

[Kea89]   Michael Kearns. *The Computational Complexity of Machine Learning*. PhD thesis, Harvard University Center for Research in Computing Technology, May 1989.

[Knu81]   D. Knuth. *The Art of Computer Programming: Volume 2, Seminumerical Algorithms*. 2nd edition, Addison-Wesley, Reading, MA, 1981.

[KO84]   Hugh Kenner and Joseph O'Rourke. A travesty generator for micros. *BYTE*, November 1984.

[Koh90]   J.T. Kohl. The use of encryption in kerberos for network authentication. In *Advances in Cryptology–CRYPTO '89 Proceedings*. Springer-Verlag, 1990.

[Kom95]   John Kominek. Convergence of fractal encoded images. In James Storer, editor, *IEEE Data Compression Conference*, pages 242–251, 1995.

[KV89]   Michael Kearns and Leslie Valient. Cryptographic limitations on learning boolean formulae and finite automata. In *Proceedings of the Twenty-First Annual ACM Symposium on Theory of Computing*, pages 433–444, Seattle, WA, May 1989.

[LJ83]   Shu Lin and Daniel J. Costello Jr. *Error Control Coding: Fundaments and Applications*. Prentice Hall, Englewood Cliffs, NJ, 1983.

[LMBO95]   Steve Low, Nicholas Maxemchuk, Jack Brassil, and Larry O'Gorman. Document marking and identification using both line and word shifting. In *Proceedings of the 1995 Conference on Infocom '95*, April 1995.

[Mei94]   W. Meier. On the security of the idea block cipher. In *Advances in Cryptology–EUROCRYPT '93 Proceedings*, 1994. Springer-Verlag.

[Mer91]   R.C. Merkle. Fast software encryption functions. In *Advances in Cryptology–CRYPTO '90 Proceedings*, 1991. Springer-Verlag.

[MNSS87]   S.P. Miller, B.C. Neuman, J.I. Schiller, and J.H. Saltzer. Section e.2.1: Kerberos authentication and authorization system. Technical report, MIT Project Athena, Dec 1987.

[NIS91]   NIST. Proposed Federal Information Processing Standard for Digital Signature Standard (DSS). 56(169), Aug 30 1991.

[NIS94]   NIST. Approval of federal information processing standards publication 186, digital signature standard (dss). *Federal Register*, 58(96), May 1994.

[NY89]   M. Naor and M. Yung. Universal one-way hash functions and their cryptographic applications. In *Proceedings of the 21nd Annual ACM Symposium on Theory of Computing*, pages 33–43. ACM, 1989.

[NY90]   M. Naor and M. Yung. Public-key cryptosystems provably secure against chosen ciphertext attacks. In *Proceedings of the 22nd Annual ACM Symposium on Theory of Computing*, pages 427–437. ACM, 1990.

[Pfi96]   Birgit Pfitzmann. Information hiding terminology. In *Information Hiding, Lecture Notes of Computer Science (1174)*, New York, Heidelberg, 1996. Springer-Verlag.

[RH96]   K.R. Rao and J.J. Hwang. *Techniques & Standards for Image, Video & Audio Coding*. Prentice Hall, Upper Saddle River, NJ, 1996.

[RSA78]   R. Rivest, A. Shamir, and L. Adleman. A method for obtaining digital signatures and public-key cryptosystems. *Communications of the ACM*, 21(2):120–126, Feb 1978.

[RSA79]   R. Rivest, A. Shamir, and L. Adleman. On digital signatures and public key cryptosystems. Technical Report MIT/LCS/TR-212, MIT Laboratory for Computer Science, Jan 1979.

[RSA83]   R. Rivest, A. Shamir, and L. Adleman. Cryptographic communications system and method. U.S. Patent #4,405,829, Sep 20 1983.

[Sch93]   Bruce Schneier. Data guardians. *MacWorld*, 10(2), Feb 1993.

[Sch94]   Bruce Schneier. *Applied Cryptography*. John Wiley and
            Sons, New York, 1994.

[Sch94]   Bruce Schneier. The Blowfish encryption algorithm. *Dr.
            Dobbs Journal*, 20(4), Apr 94.

[Sha97]   James Harold Shaw. *Information Theoretic Protection for In-
            tellectual Property*. PhD thesis, Princeton University, 1997.

[Sim84]   G.J. Simmons. The prisoner's problem and the subliminal
            channel. In *Advances in Cryptology: Proceedings of CRYPTO
            '83*. Plenum Press, 1984.

[Sim85]   G.J. Simmons. The subliminal channel and digital sig-
            natures. In *Advances in Cryptology: Proceedings of EURO-
            CRYPT 84*. Springer-Verlag, 1985.

[Sim86]   G.J. Simmons. A secure subliminal channel (?). In *Advances
            in Cryptology–CRYPTO '85 Proceedings*. Springer-Verlag,
            1986.

[Smi93]   M.E. Smid. The DSS and the SHS. In *Federal Digital Signa-
            ture Applications Symposium*, Rockville, MD, Feb 1993.

[SNS88]   J.G. Steiner, B.C. Neuman, and J.I. Schiller. Kerberos:
            An authentication service for open network systems. In
            Usenix Conference Proceedings, Feb 1988.

[SOSL94]   Marvin Simon, Jim Omura, Robert Scholtz, and
            Barry Levitt. *Spread Spectrum Communications Handbook*.
            McGraw-Hill, New York City, 1994.

[Sto88]   James Storer. *Data Compression*. Computer Science Press,
            Rockville, MD, 1988.

[TD96]   Bo Tao and Bradley Dickinson. Adaptive watermarking
            in the dct domain. *Pre-Print*, 1996.

[Val84]   Leslie G. Valient. A theory of the learnable. *Communica-
            tions of the ACM*, 27:1134–1142, 1984.

[Way88]   Peter Charles Wayner. A redundancy reducing cipher.
            Cryptologia, 12(2), April 1988.

[Way92]   Peter C. Wayner. Content-addressable search engines and
          DES-like systems. In *Advances in Cryptology: CRYPTO '92
          Lecture Notes in Computer Science, volume 740*, pages 575–
          586, New York, 1992. Springer-Verlag.

[Wie93]   M.J. Wiener. Efficient DES key search. Technical Report
          TR-244, School of Computer Science, Carleton University,
          May 1993.

[Wol96]   Stephen Wolfram. *The Mathematica Book*. Wolfram Media
          and Cambridge University Press, Champaign, IL, 1996.

Index

Related Titles from AP Professional

AHUJA, *Network and Internet Security*

AHUJA, *Secure Commerce on the Internet*

CAMPBELL/CAMPBELL, *World Wide Web Pocket Directory*

CASEY, *The Hill on the Net*

CRANE, *Mutual Fund Investing on the Internet*

FEILER, *Cyberdog*

FISHER, *CD-ROM Guide to Multimedia Authoring*

FOLEY, *The Microsoft Exchange Guide*

GRAHAM, *TCP/IP Addressing*

KEOGH, *Webmaster's Guide to VB Script*

LEVINE, *Live Java*

LEVITUS/EVANS, *Cheap and Easy Internet Access (Windows Version)*

LEVITUS/EVANS, *Cheap and Easy Internet Access (Macintosh Version)*

LOSHIN, *TCP/IP for Everyone*

LOSHIN, *TCP/IP Clearly Explained*

MURRAY/PAPPAS, *The Visual J++ Handbook*

OZER, *Publishing Digital Video*

OZER, *Video Compression for Multimedia*

PAPPAS/MURRAY, *Java with Borland C++*

PFAFFENBERGER, *Netscape Navigator 3.0 (Macintosh Version)*

PFAFFENBERGER, *Netscape Navigator 3.0 (Windows Version)*

PFAFFENBERGER, *Publish it on the Web! (Macintosh Version)*

PFAFFENBERGER, *Publish it on the Web! (Windows Version)*

PFAFFENBERGER, *Netscape Navigator Gold*

PFAFFENBERGER, *The Elements of Hypertext Style*

RIBAR, *The Internet with Windows 95*

SCHENGILI-ROBERTS, *The Advanced HTML Companion*

SINCLAIR/HALE, *Intranets vs. Lotus Notes*

SULLIVAN, *Using Internet Explorer to Browse the Internet*

TITTEL/ROBBINS, *E-Mail Essentials*

TITTEL/ROBBINS, *Internet Access Essentials*

VACCA, *JavaScript Development*

VACCA, *VRML: Bringing Virtual Reality to the Internet*

VAUGHAN-NICHOLS, *Intranets*

WATKINS/MARENKA, *The Internet Edge in Business*

WAYNER, *Agents at Large*

WAYNER, *Disappearing Cyrptography*

WAYNER, *Java and JavaScript Programming*

WAYNER, *Digital Cash, 2/e*

Ordering Information

 **AP PROFESSIONAL**
An imprint of ACADEMIC PRESS
A division of HARCOURT BRACE & COMPANY

ORDERS (USA and Canada): 1-800-3131-APP or APP@acad.com
AP Professional Orders: 6277 Sea Harbor Dr., Orlando, FL 32821-9816

Europe/Middle East/Africa: 0-11-44 (0) 181-300-3322
Orders: AP Professional 24-28 Oval Rd., London NW1 7DX

Japan/Korea: 03-3234-3911-5
Orders: Harcourt Brace Japan, Inc., Ichibancho Central Building 22-1, Ichibancho Chiyoda-Ku, Tokyo 102

Australia: 02-517-8999
Orders: Harcourt Brace & Co., Australia, Locked Bag 16, Marrickville, NSW 2204 Australia

Other International: (407) 345-3800
AP Professional Orders: 6277 Sea Harbor Dr., Orlando, FL 32821-9816

Editorial: 1300 Boylston St., Chestnut Hill, MA 02167 (617) 232-0500

Web: http://www.apnet.com/approfessional